I0080155

UNCLE B. PUBLICATIONS

INDIANAPOLIS

Nothing is Sacred

A Collection of Poetry

Robert Ragan

Nothing is Sacred

First Printing, June 2024

©2024 by Robert Ragan

All rights reserved. No part of this poetry collection may be reproduced without express written permission of the publisher. The publisher may be reached at:

unclebpublications@gmail.com

The thoughts, ideas, opinions, people, and situations presented in this book are the sole inventions of the author. Any similarities to any persons or situations living or dead, past or present, is purely coincidental.

Cover design by Paul Warren

ISBN: 978-1-957034-49-2

This edition ©2024 Uncle B. Publications, LLC

Praise for Nothing Is Sacred:

Robert Ragan is a fantastic storyteller with a refreshingly bold and unique poetic voice. Like his previous works, Nothing is Sacred presents modern problems and struggles in ways that are very personal, gritty, raw, brutal, and painfully honest. Whether writing about his battles with addiction, love found and lost, mental health challenges or when revealing other intimate aspects of his life – past and current - Ragan's latest offering provides his readers with a variety of experiences; some surrounded by regret, some self-reflective, while others expose profound moments surrounded by beauty.

- Jimmy Broccoli
author of *Damaged*, *Boy*, *Rabbits*
and the upcoming collection *Failure*

Robert Ragan's poetry is a gut-level exploration of life and love. The down-and-out, the winners and losers, and those just trying to survive all find their way into his poems. Each one takes the reader through life's dark places as well as those perfect moments. Ragan gets real about relationships, poverty, addiction, love, loss, and hope, and each poem is an emotional journey. His work stays with the reader and doesn't let go.

- Margot Kinberg
crime fiction author of
the Joel Williams series and
the Patricia Stanley series.

Nothing Is Sacred

Destroy Everything

Where do you go
What do you do
When the pick you up
Sends you down and
Something in your
Brain is wired
To make it too tough
To just say No
It's the mind rewired
To not care
And destroy everything
No hunger to create
Time just flies
As I make myself sick
Disgusted by
Where all those hours went
Wish I'd crossed those wires
Put everything back
Where it needs to be
But no I'm gonna always
Battle the need
The need to not care
At the time it doesn't
Feel like I've destroyed anything
But when it's over
It makes me wish I was dead
Suicidal all the time
But this is beyond
Wanting to take your own life
So what do you do
Where do you go
When the pick you up
Leaves you feeling lower

Than rock bottom
You do it all over again
Rewire your mind
To not give a fuck
And destroy everything

2 Nothing Is Sacred

Dream To The Knocking

I lay down
With another whore
While you slept deeply
No, I said
You should both be
Sleeping to my left and right
Awaken by addicts
Banging on my doors
And windows at night
Oh, they just want to borrow
Ten or twenty bucks
Shit I'm broke
I can't help em
And believe me
They'll knock all night
Not leaving empty handed
No, I said
I'd love to knock
One of em the fuck out
I can't stand it
Nowhere to go but
I spend half my life
Pretending I'm not at home
Oh, the sledgehammer fantasies
Blood that seems so real
It makes you cringe
I'm not at home
I'm never coming home again
Now get the fuck off my lawn
Before I call the cops
Yeah, you're right
I'd never do that

I don't have it in me to tell
Besides if I did
I'd end up having a warrant
And we'd all go to jail

4 Nothing Is Sacred

When Everything Became Sacred

For years I heard your name
I'm sure we crossed paths
In that old pool hall where
We all used to hang out as teens
I probably even spoke
But never got to know you
Still for years I heard your name
Then you popped up in
People you may know
Turns out you were a painter
Sometimes a poetess
Always in love with the arts
I love them too
With all my heart
So I had this fantasy
About us being an artistic power couple
I'd heard your name
Throughout circles for years
Turns out you were a legend
Then everything became sacred
Outspoken...
You'd rather no one bother you
When you're out smoking
But I'd blow you up all the time
Why not when I spent weekends with you
Thought we were together
Thought you were mine
I will never forget the first night
After the heated passion
Laying there with you in my arms
With your head on my chest
Sleeping Goddess

Robert Ragan 5

Sent me into Astral Projection
As I left my body and
Floated to the ceiling
Looking down at you
Laying there peacefully
In my arms
With your head on my chest
After that your Sacred Name
Was carved into my soul
And no matter what
I'd always have a part of you
Only it wasn't enough
I had to have all of you
You had every bit of me
The morning after
I left my body
Did you not say
You felt something
When I touched you
Did you not say that
I had electric fingertips
Ultimately I tried
To hold on too tight
Not all soulmates are lovers
It was hard but I learned to accept that
After you everything was so intense
Every poetry groupie
Became another Sacred Name
Still it was you
It was always you
Why else...
Did I hear your name for years

6 Nothing Is Sacred

Do Or Dark

Mental health days
Putting bills off
Didn't realize I was
Digging a hole for myself
The whole time
Sometimes it seems
Like all I have
Is my soul
Being I don't know
How to sell mine
 Slow down
Is what I would tell time
But there's no
Talking my way
Out of this one
Funny how I kept
Avoiding all these problems
Now I'm not any stronger
But still have to face them
All at one time
No it's not funny
As a matter of fact
I'm worried sick
I've just got to do
What I should have
Been doing all along
Only now everything's worse
Since I've been
Doing it all wrong
All I can do now
Is take a deep breath
Times not going to slow down

Robert Ragan 7

I just have to make sure
I'm ahead when
That day comes

8 Nothing Is Sacred

Doesn't Matter Where

So many times
I've thought to myself
Wish I could save
Up the money
Get my license back
Buy a car
Leave and never
Come back to NC ever again
Might not see him
But I'm not going anywhere
As long as my son is here
Definitely won't see him
But at least we still talk
His older sister
Well I'm here if she
Ever stops hating me
Sometimes I think to myself
I'm not in either one of their lives
So why not get out of here
And try to save my own life
Really that's the dumbest joke
I've ever heard
Doesn't matter where I go
You can bet your ass
Trouble isn't far behind
And if it doesn't follow
I'll be sure to find it
Wherever I go
I'll become acquainted
With all the drug dealers there
Along with all the other
Addicts and low lives in the area

Robert Ragan 9

What I'm trying to say is
There's no hope for me
Houses are never haunted
No they're haunted by the people
Who move in and bring
Their demons along
Try to tell myself
I'm just being paranoid
But I know
There's people
Out to get me
Everywhere we go
We all bring our demons along
Fuck with me
If you want to
Just be mindful
That I bring a mind full
Full of shit

10 Nothing Is Sacred

Talk With The Dark

I've listened to you
For long enough
In my head
I hear every word
Take every message to heart
Well now it's time
For you to listen to me
Gonna perform a self exorcism
In this bitch
If I bring you to the flesh
Will you listen to me then
First of all
You're gonna leave me alone
You're gonna shut the fuck up
Unless you have something helpful
At least something positive to say
I need a voice in my head telling me
Come on man
Everything is going to be ok
You just need to get up go to work
And face the day
Billers on my ass
I'll never be free of them
Staying at home
Listening to you
In my head
Talking about just
Get some shit
Do it and od
We know you don't
Have it in you
To slit your wrist again

Robert Ragan 11

Hanging is a new option
But you said
You didn't think
I could go through
With that either
For once I can say
You were right about that shit
And I'm not about
To intentionally overdose
If I go out fucked up
Just know I died laughing
I'd be free of all this shit
Smiling like accidents happen
By the way
What happens to you
If I up and decide
To kill myself
Guess you gonna move on
Like I never existed
And start talking to someone else
No sir no way
You done got in the
Wrong mind this time
Before it's over
I'm gonna make you
Believe in me
You're gonna be like
When he was down
I offered him in the rope
Not to pull him up
No to hang himself with
Hate it but now
There's all this hope
Bitch the light

12 Nothing Is Sacred

Ain't even started shining yet
In my head
I hear every word
Take every message to heart
Well from now on
You're gonna listen to me
I call all the shots
I take all the shots
All my hope
All my will to live
Nothing you can say
Will ever take it away again
I'm gonna make you
Believe in me

You Two

When it feels like
They're closing in
When it feels like
They're about to
Eat me alive
I try to think about you two
I can't let em get me
Because someday
I have to do a lot more
For both of you
Spent my life chasing dreams
But you two are apart of me
And deserve everything
In this life
I have to give
Should have been
Tucking you in
Telling you
I'd never let
The monsters hurt you
But I didn't
Now look at us years later
I think of you two
When the monsters are after me
When it feels like
They're closing in
When it feels like
They've taken all my hope
I try to think about you two
I can't let em get me
I've got to be here
For both of you

14 Nothing Is Sacred

No not only be here
Be a better father too

Do This For Fun

Have the upmost respect
For some of the writers
In your clique
You're the one I laugh at
Say you ain't shit
Analyzing you
I could
Pick apart your hypocrisy
Right here
Turn your day dreams
Into a fucking nightmare
Boy dem lips done touched the masses
Got to be chapped from kissing
All those asses
Trying to make a name for yourself
But really you should be ashamed of yourself
Wrote this just for fun
Next time I might actually
Get real with it
No, I hate you
But not that bad
Not going to shed any light
Hey, I'm hiding in the dark too
Just remember don't ever
Fuck with me again
Cause I can make the dark
A Hell of a lot darker

16 Nothing Is Sacred

One Of Those Names On The Cover

We had some wild times
I mean we got
Fucked up Fucked up
I loved you with a passion
My time with you
I can still see it all clear
It was one of the best
Times of my life
But I mean I
Fucked it all up
Sorry you were just irresistible
My hunger for you beyond insatiable
I mean I couldn't
Get enough of you
And that was enough
To fuck it all up
Can't ever have you again
But I still love you with a passion
Why? Because you're the realest
And one of my best friends
In the world to this day
Swamped with your own life
But you take the time
To talk to me
You pull for me to get sober
And I mean
That means
Everything to me

Robert Ragan 17

Christmas In The Gutter

Another broke ass Christmas
Wait didn't I win
That five hundred dollar
Cash prize last year
I did but at the time
My lights were about
To get disconnected
If I didn't come up
With about six fitty
This year the light bill
Is lower but I'm still
Worried about how
I'm gonna pay it
Not only that
How am I going to send
My kids money for Christmas
Might get something might not
If daddy is responsible for the wishlist
On top of all that
How am I going to afford
Weed pills and cigarettes
Yeah let's get real
What's more important
Getting high
My kids
Or the fucking light bill
Hopefully I can take care of it all
But at least I can proudly say
I'll do without my highs
If that's what it comes down to
As I wrote that my mind was like
Really now Robert

18 Nothing Is Sacred

We are supposed to be
Getting real here right
If I'd just
Handled my business
Like a man is supposed to
Then I wouldn't be in this situation
Let's just say someone's get up and go
Got up and got the fuck outta here
Laying on the floor
I'm still too scared
To get up and face the day
So I have no one
To blame but myself
Oh I'll tell the kids
I'm so fucked up
In the head mentally
I can't even get up
And go to work
Trust me they know they know
At times in my life
I've been stronger
On my feet
I'd love for them
To see me there again
For now I fear the worst
Thinking of everything
Under the sun
That could possibly go wrong
And this is why I hate Christmas

Robert Ragan 19

When Your Wings Heal

Who was your mother
Who was your father
Put them together
And what do you have
A masterpiece in
Flesh and blood
You're such a hopeless romantic
They must have been so in love
Who was my trainor
Who was my master
That's how my parents
Made me feel
But that feeling isn't real
It's not real
So here I am
It's me
All I am
You aren't stuck
With what you've got
You're free to walk away
You're free to stay away
Of course I'm going
To beg you
To come back
But it doesn't mean
You have to
Alone in the shadows now
The demon wears a halo
As to try and fool me
I feel like they're
Going to get me soon
Conquer me

20 Nothing Is Sacred

Kill me
Just wanted to say
I love you
Before they do

It Was From The Broken Heart

Almost twenty-one
Hope i didn't
Make my daughter
Look like an
Angsty teenage drama queen
She is far from that
She's a far better person
Than me in all aspects of life
Like I said She's a writer like me
Only she takes her time
Torturing herself over sentences
The way I believe a writer should
I torture myself but
Mainly let it all fly
For the editor to do all the dirty work
Anyway this has been bothering me
Last thing I want to do
Is use my own flesh and blood for a gimmick
That goes for my son too and
Everything I ever wrote about him
My mother and father as well

22 Nothing Is Sacred

Self-Defeating Prophecy

Counting curses
Fascinated by the dark side
Got my Scrupulosity acting up
Is art worth
Burning in Hell
For all eternity
Once had this feeling
That the gates of Heaven
Would never open for me
If I die without
Burning all those notebooks
A pastor told me
Son if you had that feeling
I'd go home and
Burn every one of em
Right now
Couldn't bring myself
To do it
Guess art's worth
Burning in Hell after all
As I live my life
Desperate to share
These curses with the world
If deep down
I feel like I should
Burn it all
Then why would I
Want to share it
With anyone else
All that talk

Robert Ragan 23

It's all destruction
The only message
Behind it
Is there's no hope
In the end
I get to burn
In a hotter fire
Being I saw the light
Plus knew the truth
Yet still gave myself
Over to my dark fascination
Art is not worth it

24 Nothing Is Sacred

Wrong Footsteps

My son failed
A drug test
At the group home
I said
If you're trying to follow
In my footsteps
Then you're on
The right track
Or the wrong
Side of it anyway
Damn this is not
What I want from him
I mean the weed
Obviously I can't
Say much about that not
When I'm smoking
Like a chimney
In this motherfucker
It's just all that other shit
That scares me
I definitely don't want
To see him on pills
Wondering if he'll
Die from a Fentanyl overdose
The same way
My favorite cousin did
No and I also
Don't ever want to see my son
Out here tweaking
On any kind of stimulants
I don't condone violence

Robert Ragan 25

Especially involving my son
But if he ever shoots anything up
I better see bullet holes
Not a fucking tract mark on his arm
When he was coming up
I thought he was going to be
An ongoing problem
An ongoing problem
I was willing to take on for him
Instead now he's the calm one
With a heart of gold
So I don't ever want him
To follow in my footsteps
No that track leads to nowhere
And he deserves a better life than that

26 Nothing Is Sacred

Not Her Please Not Her

My daughter tells me
That her life is over and
She's thinking about
Killing herself
Just hearing this
I cringe and panic
I literally cannot stand it
I want to help but
There's nothing I can do
I'm her father
She should be able
To turn to me
But I'm barely
Taking care of myself
All I can offer is my voice
She can always talk to me
I think back to all those
Trips to institutions and
Psychiatric wards
I'm sure my parents cringed
I know they panicked
Overdoses
Slit wrists
At least I haven't
Went through all that
But everything I
Put my parents through
Seems like it's all coming back
She's my daughter
A writer like me
All I want is

Robert Ragan 27

For her to be okay.

28 Nothing Is Sacred

Just Thinking

About you
Yeah I still
Think about you
All the time
Devote so much thought
But I'm never on your mind
Like some of these writers
I want to be down with them
I want to fit in
But to them I don't even exist
Do I even exist
As far as you're concerned
Damn I hope so
Because I think about you all the time
Honestly you're probably
Thinking about someone else
If there's anyone out there
Feeling ignored while
Thinking about me
Please hit me up
I don't want to make anyone
Feel unimportant
Yes I know that
Nobody's thinking about me
Just saying just in case
About you
My mind turns flips
In a wonderland of confusion
The only thing clear
Is that we are
Not meant to be

Robert Ragan 29

I guess I'll try
To write myself
Out of this rabbit hole
For the rest of my life
Thinking
Just thinking
About you
Just thinking about
The outcast
The In Crowd
Just thinking about it all
Hating myself
Because it's all my fault
If I wasn't me
If I was someone else
I'd be accepted
I'd be loved by you
Just thinking about it
Gives me chills

30 Nothing Is Sacred

Spoken Word Sundays

Smoked out the parking lot
Did a little bump in the bathroom
Got on the mic and stumbled
Through my lines
While reading them off paper
After that I said
No more getting high
Before I go up
To read my poetry
Focused I read perfectly
People in the crowd
Came up to me afterwards
And said my poetry
Hit them really hard
Satisfied with my performance
I celebrated by going outside
With a couple of other poets
And smoking out the parking lot
Then I went in the bathroom
And snorted a fat line
Before going back upstairs
To listen to the other poets

I Can Judge You Too

Hate to do it
But I gotta talk
To another soul
What happened to you
When your boys were scrapping
Inside the Hideout Bar&Grill
They were in there
Swinging pool sticks
And you just up and split
Even had the nerve to call
Thirty minutes later
Talking about you were
Just checking on em
After that move nobody
Wants to hear about the fights
You've been in
Talking tough all that bragging shit
You never did none of that
You bumped your head and imagined it
Yeah after that move
Definitely don't speak
On your loyalty anymore
And how you had so and so's back
Motherfucker you were
Pulling for em from the car
And got the nerve
To talk shit about me
I hardly even know those dudes
And I would have been
Throwing chairs and
Swinging pool sticks right with em
You're too pussy to fight

32 Nothing Is Sacred

Thinking about your dance moves
Hoping you got the right rhythm
If you're wondering if this is poisonous
Bitch you're dealing with straight venom
As a matter of fact
Ever since that night
I heard they don't
Invite you over
As often as they used to
I wonder why that is
Really I figured all of you would run
You know turn into bitches
But no just you
After that move
You burned quite a few bridges
But you wanted to cross em
The short way
That's why I'm pleased that
I'm about to say
I came up struggling
You're only out
Was the easy way
In closing don't even think my name
Yet alone write it or speak it out loud
No telling the kind of bad energy
That could bring you
No that's right
You're the subliminal boy
Thinking you're going
Over someone's head
But I got the message
Loud and clear
What you had to say

Robert Ragan 33

Bitch you can't play keyboard warrior
When I know where the fuck you stay

34 Nothing Is Sacred

Learn Someday

Say they got your back
Yeah when they
Stab you in it
All I got is me
Family fake
Friends fake
Lovers are snakes
Maybe I'll learn someday
Can't give as much as others
But I give what I can
Should be selfish
Like everyone else
Maybe I'll learn someday
Not to take anyone's word
Not to depend on anyone but me
Stop showing everyone else love
For once love myself
Can't depend on anyone but me
Maybe I'll learn someday
Say they want me to be happy
But don't really give a fuck about me
It's not their fault they lie
It's my fault for believing that bullshit
Maybe I'll learn someday
Such an old soul
Longing for someone who really cares
 I'll probably never learn
Yeah I'll always play someone's fool

Small Town Up All Night

Heard this dope dealer say
I'm not staying up all night
I said you better stay up
Talking about going to sleep
You better hope
You hear that tapping at the window
At 3am
If not I bet there's something
Sketchy going on while you're snoozing
Can't make a killing in the dream world
The fiends are up all night and you're losing
Knew this one couple
They we're both
Unemployed heads
Doing odd jobs
For the plug to
Get a twenty bag
Coming down
The guy showed up
At the man's door
Asked if he needed
Any yard work done
The man said No
With tears in his eyes
Ol boy was a ginger with a bowl cut
Looking like a red headed member of the Beatles
Voice shaking and quivering he asked
You got any dishes that need washing
Any clothes that need folding
I'm not too ashamed to fold
You or your wife's underwear
He would have said

36 Nothing Is Sacred

I'll get my girlfriend to suck your dick
But she wouldn't do that
Hell he wanted to say
I'll suck your dick
But for some reason he didn't
Instead he walked back
To his mom's trailer
Fingers digging in his mop
Itching scratching at his braincells
His girl was like
Oh he ain't got
No work for us to do
Well since he wants
To shut down shop
And go to sleep at night
Well he'll have some work
For us to do tomorrow
In that relationship
She wore the pants
And was the brains of the operation
The only brain as a matter of fact
Speaking of brains and operations
Her boyfriend should
Have got a lobotomy
That night the two of them
Walked their dogs
Around the trailer park
Just like they always do
She just happened
To suggest they
Walk em over by
The dopeman's trash outside
Man them mutts

Robert Ragan 37

Tore that shit all to Hell
The next day Red Beatle
Showed up like he didn't
See the trash outside scattered everywhere
He asked hey you got any work to do
Cold blooded he said
You should call the pound
On the Goddamn neighbors dogs
I can't believe them bastards
Tore up all your trash like that
He was happy to run back to his mom's
And tell his girlfriend
They could clean up the plugs yard
For a twenty bag of dope
He stood there looking stupid
While she used the rake
And done most of the work
Bet your ass afterwards
He wanted to do most of the dope
Believe me when I tell you
There's some sorry
Motherfuckers around here
Ain't none of us
Got no hope
The fiends gonna end up
Brain dead or all the way dead
The dealers are gonna
End up in prison
Nothing about this life
Ever leads to anything positive
Every road has a dead end
Fentanyl killing all the nod heads
Most of them have a dead friend
So let me repeat myself again

38 Nothing Is Sacred

Nothing about this life
Ever leads to anything positive
All of it will take you
To places you don't
Want to go
Not to mention
Along the way
You'll lose
Everyone you know
But if you must live this life
Your ass better stay up all night

Her Heart Is Golden

You said No sad faces
When I replied
To your message
But those sad faces
Express a happiness
So deep I can't explain it
You already got to me
When you said
I'll always be
Your friend no matter what
But then you said
Literally no matter what ok
That time I felt something
That left me in chills
When I feel that I know it's real
When I feel that I start going crazy
Thinking about all the names
How could I ever
Put one above yours
The Queen would have
Never been faithful to me
While I was locked up
There's so much you've
Done for me
That no one else
Would ever do
Had to let me go
But you're the only one
Who never completely
Just threw me away
So I should have never
Put anyone else above you

40 Nothing Is Sacred

My life is so fucked up
I know I don't have a chance
But I hope you do know I love you
You will always be the
Realest One I Ever Loved
Might share broken bones
With other hearts
But titanium is the only truth
Okay sorry just wanted
To say all that
Don't think I'm all crazy
Falling in love with you again
I can't cause I've been in love with you
I just know we can never be again
I guess I just put my heart into being a friend
I know you don't need me
The way that I need you
But if you ever do
I will always be your friend no matter what
Literally no matter what ok

Robert Ragan 41

Gutterest Adventures

This motherfucker
I took him with me
One time to meet the connect
Bitch in there
Calling him the plug
Asking questions like
You ever worry about
Getting knocked
Dude gave me a weird look
Passed the blunt
Then told my buddy
You damn right
I worry about getting knocked
Why you asking
You the fucking police or something
I literally had to give up
That gorilla glue blunt
And get my boy the fuck outta there
He didn't know it
But he was probably
About to get pistol whipped
In that bitch
Motherfucker fucked up my connect
I ain't been able to go back ever since
On the way home I asked him
Why the fuck would you
Bring up some shit like that
Oh I know
You want to sound
Cool and hard
Like you know something
You need to

42 Nothing Is Sacred

Shut the fuck up
Cause you don't know shit
That's why you never
Take this guy with you
Tell his ass
To walk to the corner store
And buy a couple of blunts
Then wait until you get back

Feast On The Queen

Dark nights
Rusted armor pierced
Gunfire
So secure upon
Your locks
But the crown drips blood
Soon the worms
Will pick your brain
Find out
The secrets of the dead
Before they begin
To pick your bones
Think about that
As you call
All the shots
Breaking
All the hearts
It all comes
To an end
Beauty fades
Sleazy magazine siren
I've had enough of your lies
It's time to tell the truth
To all the liars
That never heard it before
Run for cover love
The dark can't save you
It's all
Coming to light

44 Nothing Is Sacred

The Crown Drips Blood

So sick of this war
We fight
Inside our heads love
Scoured this place
So hard to find peace
When this town is damned
Hold me love
Push me face down
Into a stream of consciousness
Drowning in words I'll dream of you
My bricks build sentences
Hidden meaning in the mortar
Let's live until we can both
Die as martyrs
That way we'll live forever
In honor actually remembered
No one else i want to stand with
But you love
If I'm destined
To crash and burn
I want you
Right there beside me
We're both sick of this war
Yet we can't help but fight
When our minds are the battlefields
We'll never find peace
Not in a town
Cursed by its secrets
We'll make it out alive
Somehow my love

Robert Ragan 45

Celebrate The End

Benefits beneath the surface
Wicked sin and we laugh
No use in letting the skin
Hold you back
Explore the possibilities
Emotions lost in the woods
Moonlight only comes
To tell the dark skies story
There are no benefits
Beneath the surface
There is no purpose
Even the lives of kings are worthless
Realized all this
While the exploring the truth
Upper echelon liars
Wear masks and
Dance around the fire
Blood sacrifice ritual
Who did you have to off to get on
All the kings are worthless
Only avoided their beheading
Because the Moonlight is gone
And they're the only ones left
To tell the dark skies story

46 Nothing Is Sacred

Almost Over

I love you
I'm sure now that
I always will
Doesn't matter
Addiction
Poverty
Hopelessness
Only those things love me
Down and out
I love you
Feeling the high
I love you
Spend all my time
In love with the fact that
I love you
Don't have you but you're all I have
Your beauty is reality
Lost my life
When I lost touch with you
Anyway just remember that
I love you
I'm sure now that
I always will
The ghost of us watches me
Fall apart after saying goodbye

Run Before We Crawl

Blazing eyes river tears
Only remember now
Not the hearts never here
Cursed by sky fantasies
I watch as
Meaningless stories unfold
Now here we are separate
Yet our spirits can't be separated
For you I'm waiting desperate
Souls longing to shout no scream
How they made it
It's a new night
No longer coming for heads
Weak shoulders
Need something to cry on them
Blazing eyes close
River tears stop racing
I'll never forget right now
With the only heart that matters
The pen is a flame thrower
Burning down brains
Between false temples
Left abandoned
In blood and the ruins
For now the new heart sings
I dream the sound
Drink it's essence
Nothing in the sky can harm us
I made up the story
So we can be happy there

48 Nothing Is Sacred

I'm Your New Therapist

Boy look at you
All dressed up
In a suit and tie
My condolences
Cause I'm sure
Someone has died
Oh you're going to court
What you facing
Man we all know
What you're repping
Let me guess
Drug charges
Burglary maybe
Assault with a
Deadly weapon
No bitch you're going to court
Because you won't work
And pay you're child support
Dude really you should be on
America's Dumbest Criminals
Talking about you're a thief
Bitch stealing candy
At the Dollar Tree doesn't count
Talk to me when you steal a couple of thou
Another thing
Yeah one more thing before I go
Motherfucker out here bragging
Talking about money and weed
What was it you said
I got a lot of green
Well while you're at it

Robert Ragan 49

Please take care
Of your personal hygiene
Every time you smile
We all suffer
Man I can't believe
It's not butter
With you're armpit sweat stains
Stinking like high heaven stranger
Not to mention you're...
Always trying to bust a sag in them Wranglers
I'm gonna shut up now
Your therapy session is over
Oh yeah and you better pay
When I bill you
I'm the only therapist you know
That will come to your house
And fucking kill you
No I'm just kidding or Am I

50 Nothing Is Sacred

But I Need You

The night trembles
When you wake up
Those eyes opened wide
They see as you study
Everything
Know you'll find
Something wrong
With what I'm doing
Every raindrop is you
My parade canceled
Said the pain got to you
Mental illness is a cancer
How can we be
When you have
So many questions
And I don't have
A single answer
We're both depressed
But you could
Bring me out of mine
But no you're always
Out of your mind
Looking at everything
You see everything
But nothing is ever
Good enough for you
I'm not good enough for you
So I want to go my own way
I just don't want to leave you behind
I know I don't have
Anything to offer but the slums

Robert Ragan 51

A shack where
I stay fucked up on pills
But you wouldn't be happy
If I offered you
A mansion in the hills
So why do I even try
You don't know
How many times
I've woke up
Wishing I'd died
The night doesn't tremble
It just stays dark

52 Nothing Is Sacred

Turn Yourselves In

On the run
Living in a hotel room
You and me
Took the bed
The 3rd wheel
Slept on the floor
And got one
Hell of a show
We fist fought
Over the idea
Of sharing you
Damn right
You're lucky
You were
Dead set
Against it
If I'd even thought
You were down
I would have
Left you two
To fuck and
Figure it out
By the way
We're out the room
In three days
Better call your
Mother and father
Hit em with the sad story
I'll write it all down
If you need me too
And whatever you do

Robert Ragan 53

Don't say anything about the cops
Everything will be fine
We're just gonna
Turn ourselves in
Like responsible adults
When we're ready
It's not like
They're gonna
Lock us up forever
Plus we're gonna have
All the Ramen noodles we want
Commissary kings in that bitch
Oh and my Queen too
Oh never mind
All that turning ourselves in talk
Motherfuckers gonna have
To come and get us
Probably catch us
Meeting up with the plug
In the Burger King parking lot
Probably get behind us
And run our bad tags at a traffic light
Oh, it's coming
They're gonna get us baby
Are you ready
Because I'm ready

54 Nothing Is Sacred

My Own Desolation Angels

Money to buy a pack
But can't get any cigarettes
If I was dead broke
I'd have a ride
To the store
If I needed it
Damn that's how life
Has been going these days
Actually it's been going this way
For a really long time
And I'm talking about things
Way worse than not having cigarettes
I'm talking withdrawals overdoses
Missing the vein hematoma queens
And wide awake icy jezzebells
Badass stoner chicks with braids
It's whatever you want on the streets
But the prices must be paid
All these people I'm talking about
It's like black clouds are drawn to them
Bad luck is waiting patiently
Following ever closely
It's like a maze
They all taste the confusion
They can't help it
They're all in a haze
A waste of the solution
All I know is they
Need whatever it is they want really bad
Said they need whatever it is
They're on really bad

Robert Ragan 55

What you need
What you want
There's choices to make
Oh and it's so sad
The look on their faces so desperate
Jack had his well these are my
Desolation Angels
Nowhere to go
Thoughts on the edge of violence
Randy just robbed
His own mother again
They had to hit Wendy
With the Narcan
To bring her back to life
We're already living in Hell
If the afterlife is any worse
Please have mercy on me God
Jack had his well
These are all my fallen
Desolation Angels
I watch over them
They watch over me
Sadly there's no hope
For any of us

56 Nothing Is Sacred

Now Nothingness

You don't remember
Telling me everything
My clothes tear stained
I told you it would all be okay
I hear lately your heart
Got the feeling again
Broke too soon
Seems like it will never mend
Well just remember
When there's no one
Else to turn to
Turn towards
These open arms
You can always
Tell me everything
What yet another love
Not as strong or deep as mine
But you really think you
Got it right this time
I care about you
So I want it
Too work out
Even if I don't
Want it to work out
It's so hard to explain
Well just remember
If it doesn't work out
You can always
Turn to me
My open arms
Are always waiting

Robert Ragan 57

You know you can
Tell me anything
No you can
Tell me everything
looking for him
With my love for you
Right there on your time-line
You scroll past it
But I understand
I could write a million poems
But there's not enough words
For me to ever
Tell you everything

58 Nothing Is Sacred

Bless Those Who Really Need It

In the past
Starving
Freezing
But I never
Asked anyone for help
Not in real life
Definitely not on fb
I really needed help
But my pride
Made me ride
Out the storm
Truly suffering
Like fuck asking
Anyone for anything
If you really need it
I think you deserve it
But some people
Take your money
While they're living
Just as good as you
Scheming ass motherfuckers
Laughing at you while
They spend your
Hard earned money
This summer suffering
In the heat
I wanted to say fuck it
Quit my job
I can see me on fb now
I can't pay my rent
But it doesn't matter

Robert Ragan 59

Because I'm about
To get kicked the fuck out
My lights and water are cut off
Spiders crawl
Out of the holes in the floor
And bite me in my sleep
None of it matters
Because I'll be on the streets soon
Bet if I said something like that
Wouldn't nobody send me shit
You want to know what's really fucked up
I have a job and I'm almost literally
Going through every bit of that truthfully
You know why I love suffering and not
Asking people for help
Why because people love telling you no
I mean there are genuine people out there
I can see it in their eyes
I can hear it in their voice
When they really want to help
And hate telling you No
Those people are the last
That breed has died
So you're lucky if you
Have someone like that
In your lives
I see some of you out there
Your giving hearts beating
While you're wearing a dunce cap
Gave out of kindness
While they laugh at how
They exploited your weakness
But hey you're stronger than them
You got up and worked hard

60 Nothing Is Sacred

To help them
So who's really fucking weak
Definitely don't think
I'm hating on people
With problems
Genuine people have problems too
I can see it in their eyes
I can hear it in their voice
When they're really struggling hard
And appreciate everything
You do for them
I wish those people the world
As broke as I am
I might send them something
It's these scammers I'm talking about
Motherfuckers capable of working
But they'd rather give you a sad story
And get you to send them money
Since ya'll love sad stories so much
I'll tell you a ton of em
And you don't have to send me a dime
All I ever asked from anyone
Was to just read something
Don't want you're money
Just spend a little bit of your time
Anyway good luck to all of you
Out there struggling
But too prideful
To ask for help
Even you scammers
No ya'll can go to Hell
Yeah like any of you care
That I'm telling ya'll to go to Hell

Robert Ragan 61

Shit you motherfuckers
Are already there

62 Nothing Is Sacred

Cool And Unusual Punishment

Are you that dumbass
Guy at your job
You try to do
Everything right but do
Everything wrong
I know it hurts
To admit that you're stupid
We've heard it all
And yes drugs
Have fried your brain
But I heard you were also
A stupid kid
Hey I know it hurts
To admit that you're
 As dumb as a rock
To stupid to pour
Piss out of a boot
But hey truth is facts
At least you're not
As dumb as you
Used to be
Out there thinking
You were a criminal
Mastermind
A criminal mastermind
You ain't got no sense
But it's not your fault
A criminal mastermind
Is that why your dumbass was
Always getting caught
In jail begging to use the phone

Robert Ragan 63

Hey calm down
No one is picking on you
You just have to admit it
Okay I'm gonna say it slowly
And you say it with me
I....Am.....Stupid
Okay let's try something else
I....Am......A Fucking DUMBASS
There you go
Now you're free
Trust me I'm stupid
Dumb as fucking piss
Hey who knew urine
Had any form of intelligence
Plus I used to make excuses too
I'm not dumb I just can't concentrate
I was stupid to fucking dumb to concentrate
Hell I even had people
Make excuses for me
You're not stupid
You're a published writer
All that writing
Doesn't mean shit
In the real world
When I have trouble
With something at work
Do you think my boss
Gives a fuck
If I'm published in a stupid book
So there you go
You're free now
You're dumb, stupid, ignorant
Now go on be proud
You slow ass goofball

64 Nothing Is Sacred

As A Result Of Mental Illness And Poverty

Boiling water
In my only pot
To piss in
Keep telling stories
Can't get anyone
To listen
This life
Feels like
I'm on a mission
Bills due
Shit falling apart
I can't pay
To get it fixed
Cause I'm an addict
And need my fix
Borrowing money
My paycheck is gone
Before I cash it
And here I am
Talking about a story
Soon I'm gonna
Tell you one
About the guy
Living in a torn down trailer
With no lights or water
It's like basketball sometimes
Gotta make it take it
Kinda makes me think
About the shake and bake shit
Might as well make
Some extra money

Robert Ragan 65

Or blow up
This piece of shit trailer
In the process
Fuck it I'll
Take a tent and
Live in the wilderness
Wifi at the local church
Pick up their signal
Hope and pray
They don't pick up
On my vibe
Playing pretend
To be a writer
On social media
While I'm freezing
Fuck this life
It's all about falling apart
Sad when waking up
Breaks your heart
Hell let it go too
Truly the only
Good part of me
As far as the mind
A shattered skull
A splattered brain
Should get rid of
All those bad thoughts
No more memories either
No more poverty poetry
No more feeling left out
Of everything
Perished while others prosper
No longer care
If that's all they

66 Nothing Is Sacred

Have to offer
Because I don't exist
So how could I
Possibly need anything
Let me go
Let death
Swallow me whole
Eat the meat
Off the bones
Drink the blood
Spit out the soul
I am nothing
My words
Laughed at
By the elite
I am nothing
Stinky socks and shoes
My dreams
Smell like defeat
And my brain
Plays it all
On repeat
Why not shatter the skull
And splatter it
Boiling water
In my only pot
To piss in
But soon
They might
Cut it off
At least that
Will take care
Of all the leaks

Robert Ragan 67

Life is Hell
Life is a bitch on her period
Hey I can be as misogynistic
As I wanna be
I earned the right
With the memories
Of two women
Constantly haunting me
Love always feeling shady
I hate ya'll but you know
I really love the ladies
Really wish I could
Take it back to the eighties
And be a forty-two year old
Writer then
Submissions in the mailbox
Get a story published
Feel like I have the game
In a headlock
Nothing big though
Was walking barefooted
In the house and stubbed
My big toe
Okay I'm just writing
Nonsense to make you laugh now
So I'm gonna go
Be peaceful and
Enjoy your life
When you feel down
Think about my life
Even read this again
If you want to
Warning if you read it
Ten times

68 Nothing Is Sacred

I come out of the poem
And haunt you
Okay I'm really gonna go this time
By the way I would never haunt you
I would come out of the poem
And try to do something
To make your life
Brighter than before

Lady Of The Sun

Older and more wise than me
I get lost in your verse
You appreciate mine as well
You just don't like when I curse
Your photos fill me with thirst
Sometimes it feels like
My heart will burst
But we are only time
And a dream
Aren't you glad
I abandoned that rhyme scheme
Enough of that and
Enough of the distance
When I sleep
You color the world
The sun shining
On your beauty
Longing the feeling
That runs through me
These veins filled
With wild wishes
They'll never come true
But we do share the stanzas
Our souls entwined in words
Forever

70 Nothing Is Sacred

Goddess Even When The Sun Goes Down

Might be dark
But I've been
Praying for your freedom
Knowing I'll never
Break the chains
And find it
In my own life
Why do you think
I say the things I do
Darling I know
My souls damned
That's why I say
Whatever I want
Because I don't
Have to answer
To no man
No ma'am
I don't
Now you say
If I read something
Like that again
You'll go away
It's like you pushing me
To completely switch
Up my style
Just understand that I won't
That doesn't mean I don't care
I don't want you to go
Funny cause it's not like you're here
My genuine Lady Of The Sun
Just wanted to show

Robert Ragan 71

That I could write a poem about you
Just for fun
And hey it ended up
Having a lot of
Feelings behind it
I'll never meet you
But I've been
Praying for your freedom
Yeah this dark soul
Chained by demons
Unable to break free
Takes the time
To wish you well
If you go away
I will still
Live in Hell
On earth

72 Nothing Is Sacred

Can't Take Anything From Me

I've already lost everything
Live from the shack in the bottom
I'm sitting in the throne
Judging all of you
Turning my nose up
Like you ain't shit
War of words ready
Word World War deadly
No I ain't got time
To respond to
Whatever it was
You said
For your sake
Better hope
I never find out
War of words ready
Word World War deadly
What does that really mean
Well it means that
You don't want to fuck with me
The Live Wire is the Wildest

Robert Ragan 73

Realest One I Ever Loved

Long before the
Names were Sacred
It was your name
Written on all the letters
Sent to me
In jail and prison
It was your name
On my mind for years
Dating my friend
When we first met
But you and I
Had all the chemistry
Then finally after searching
For someone to truly love me
I did get a happy ending
It was the beginning of us
When you found me online
And messaged me
Out of the blue
It was finally my time
To be with you
Only I didn't know
How to handle
True love from
Someone as real as you
I'll never forget the day
I got out of prison
You were waiting
On the other side
Of the gate
Wearing that short
Hot pink dress

74 Nothing Is Sacred

Of course
You were amazing
But more than
The sins we committed
You were saving me
Saving me from the world
Saving me from myself
So obsessed
Your heart and soul
Were Sacred
As well as your name
You really loved me
So obsessed
You saved me from the world
You saved me from myself
But had no one to save you
From the burning intensity
Of my love
Wanted you so much
My time finally came
But I wanted so much more
All the time
Never mind
Life and responsibilities
I could have stayed with you
In bed forever
My hunger ruined our love
To this day I think back
Regretting how I managed
To fuck up something...
So true
Something...
So real

Robert Ragan 75

Something...
I wanted for so long
To this day
You're still in my life
You forgave me
And you listen as I
Go on and on
About my life
And how my
Heart is broken
Further away yourself now
But you still try to save me
It was my fault
I lost you
My fault
I lost this one
My fault
I lost that one
Poetically
Crying tears
Begging for love
When I'm the one
Who pushes everyone away
Guess I don't know
How to handle True Love
From someone real
So all the paths
Along my journey
Will be paved in hurt
Until I'm gone

76 Nothing Is Sacred

A Simp Love Story

Texts not returned
I just told myself
I was being overbearing
It couldn't be
That you didn't like me
After all
You used to text back
You were
The one who invited me over
No wait
After that is when
You seemed
To lose all interest
It went right over my head
But if it hadn't
I probably couldn't
Have let myself believe it
If so I'd have told myself
She cares about me
I just care about her so much
I'm driving her crazy
Couldn't help it
When it drove me crazy not to.
I just kept making all
These excuses for you
Eventually I thought
She's trying to push me away
And doesn't care
If I go away as silently as possible
No no no that's couldn't be
You had to really care about me

Robert Ragan 77

Maybe you just couldn't
Show your feelings
The way I showed mine
It all stopped
That one night
I was supposed
To get dropped off
At your place after work
Night shift
Couldn't ruin it
I was wide awake
Until you canceled at midnight
No I wasn't stalking you
Had to pass your house
On the way to my place
Laughing joking with
My friends around 3 A.M
Until we passed by
And I saw a car in your yard
That I didn't recognize
Plus your bedroom light on
I just kept making all
These excuses for you
But not that time
I got home broke the mirror
And cut myself with the glass
I wanted to call you
Ruin whatever it was
You had with him
Whoever he was...But
In the ultimate simp behavior
I pretended it didn't happen
As if I rode by seen
No car in your yard

78 Nothing Is Sacred

No light on in your bedroom
I felt if I called you out on it
You would leave me
And even if you cheated
And never cared about me
I still cared about you
And still couldn't bare to lose you
I kept sending texts
You stopped replying for even longer
Weeks went by without seeing you
Then we had a date
And you canceled it
Again I wasn't stalking you
Had to pass your house
To drive into town
Yeah you canceled our date
But your yard was filled with cars
Every light on
This time I sent you
A text the very next morning
Finally took up for myself
And that's all it took
To drive you away
Oh you texted back quick
To tell me we were over
I remember reading it
With tears rolling
Down my cheeks
Alternate ending #1
I asked to see you again
Knowing I was already
Talking to someone else
That night after you fell asleep

Robert Ragan 79

I lay there in your bed
And text her and
Check out the nude pics she sent
Alternate ending #2
I never do get over you
And write heartbreaking
Little simp poems about you
For the rest of my days

You Inspired The Dark

All alone here now
Thinking back
To what we used to be
Bones all that's left
Of our love
Scattered in the leaves
Remember that poem
Of yours that I loved
I loved everything
You ever did in art
I knew it all come
From your heart
Why did we
Have to fall apart
I loved everything
About you with
All my heart
But now all that's left of us
Is bones
The leaves burned
Turned to ashes
Look at me inspired
By your words
Living off them
When that poem wasn't even about me
You never felt the same
So now all that's left of us is a memory
That you don't even remember
Even I can't think of
What month we met
But I'm sure it was in the summer

Robert Ragan 81

Bet you thought I was
Going to say December
To Hell with it all
To Hell with everything
We're a rare breed
They don't make em
Like us anymore
As soulmates we should
Probably stick together
Only we're just
The same old story
I love you but
You're gone forever
Doesn't matter because
You're still with me
You're always with me
We live on
In the scattered pieces of my heart
We're alive and well
Creating our art
Not dead and in Hell
With all that hate in our hearts
Can you feel it
When I think about us so much
I'm actually living it
I'm with you
Whether you like it or not
You just block me out
Well the bones rest
Somewhere in the woods near you
The leaves blow in the wind
Covered by my blood
Wanted you to see
Everything I ever did

82 Nothing Is Sacred

But more than anything
I wanted to show you all my love

Robert Ragan 83

Failed The Ones Who Matter Most

Cried when
I seen your faces
Women come and go
But you two
Would always be there
I know I should have
Been there too
I am now
As much as I can be
All alone now
Messed up everything
Know sometimes
You can't stand me
I can't stand myself either
Now days it all makes sense
I was never there
When it mattered
So my time now
Means nothing
To you two
I just as well not exist
When I'm there
I'm just there
When I'm gone
I'm not missed
But I've been
missing both of you
For so long
Wishing I'd been more responsible
Wishing I'd been a better father but...
It's been way too late
For far too long

84 Nothing Is Sacred

Put Myself Through It All

God won't put more on me
Than I can bare
Not more than
I can handle right
Must be the devil then
Cause I feel more on me
Than I can bare to handle tonight
No I put it all on myself
Everything that torments me
Is ultimately all my fault
With all the problems
I forced behind me
I can exorcize them all
On the page
Yeah that's what I thought
But what if it's
Too terrifying
To even write about
What do I do then
Where on earth do I turn
That's the question
But the answer is
There's no where to turn
All I can do
Is talk to God
Hope that he forgives me
I know he does
Because none of this
Has killed me yet
Not the slit wrists
Not the intentional overdose attempts

Robert Ragan 85

None of it
Not the shotgun barrel to my forehead
Or my big toe on the trigger
Well obviously he talked
Me out of doing that one
Anyway tonight
After all the others
There's a new demon in my head
Born from recent memories
I can't kill it with my words
So allow me to fight it
With your word

86 Nothing Is Sacred

Missed Out On Me

Soft side right
This side gets passionate
This side starts fires
Don't you forget it
It's all love
Wish you all the best
But you know
You missed out
On me right
Yeah even with all my problems
I'm a good dude
I have a really good heart
And I put it all on the line
To take care of what I call mine
Yeah you feel it
You should
All that intensity
It must have been
Too much for you
I hope you find
Exactly what you want
Just always remember
You are the one I wanted
That feeling has died now
But I'd still do anything to help you
See me in my jeans and hoodie
Don't go having second thoughts now
Yeah you feel it
You like the intensity don't lie
Maybe it's too much for you
But I can see

Robert Ragan 87

You're thinking about giving it a try
Don't you know
The stars shine brighter
On the wrong side of the tracks
Maybe you should
Keep playing it safe
Cause once we go there
We can never take it back
I'm good just wanted
To put these words out there
I know you can feel it
Resist it because it's dark
And there's never going to be light
Despite all the darkness
I would have made the
Sun shine for you
So you know
You missed out on me right
Yeah you know it
But it's okay
That world was never
Meant to be explored by us

88 Nothing Is Sacred

Backs Through The Wall

Don't really know
Where to go from here
As far as my plans
Well the monkey wrench
Nearly beat me
Half to death
I only have
One thing left
And that's my job
So take it all
Once I don't have that
The rest of my life
Will crumble
And fall apart
Just take it all
Once I have nothing
There is nothing else
Anyone can take from me
It's all just a pile of junk
Without all of it I'll be free
All my cats in the pound
Every book burned
Guess I can have
The clothes on my back
Or do you want them to
You can have it all take it all
When there's nothing
Left of me but ashes
Chop it up
With the boys
Snort what's left of me

Robert Ragan 89

You'll be fucked up
Just wait
And see
Just make sure
To take it all
Every bit
Of me
For I am
The lowest
Of the low
King Scumbag
Sinners flesh
Devoured slowly
You can read this shit
But you don't really know me
For those cursed
To be apart of my life
Just know I'm bringing
Fire and brimstone
The day I can't
Go back to my job
They'll be hardly nothing left
Gonna make it even tougher
But come on please
Take it all
So I can show how dark
My true colors really are

90 Nothing Is Sacred

Birthday Cake

Everything had to be perfect
It was my daughter's birthday
I had the party set up
Bought the presents
Hokie Pokie Elmo
I knew she would love it
Bought all the food
Including the birthday cake
Happy Birthday Miranda May
Written in blue icing
On the all white
Yellow layer cake
We all ate pizza
Of course I stepped out
And hit the bowl
Knocked it out
I walked back in
Ready to let her blow out candles
Then I would cut the cake
When I went to pick it up
I saw two ants marching
Across the top of the box
Panic filled my veins
With instant static
In my head I already knew it
Before I raised the lid
Ants were all over
My daughter's birthday cake
I had the party set up
Everything was perfect
Until these ants completely

Robert Ragan 91

Fucked everything up
I was devastated
She barely cared
So excited to open presents
That memory has been
repressed for years
This week it came back to haunt me
Hopefully this sends this demon
To its prison in the back of my mind
I remember lyrics
To Maryland Mansons
The Man That You Fear
Ants are in the sugar
Yes they are
Feasting on my chance
To finally do something
Nice for my daughter
On top of all this
I think about my son
No party set up for him
Perfect wouldn't set foot
Into our lives
And he had to suffer for it.
All I ever wanted
Was the best
For both of them
Funny coming
From one of the
Worst fathers ever

92 Nothing Is Sacred

The Dark Verses Reality

Traveling out of town for work
Everyone else had a suit case
While I carried all my clothes
In a black trash bag
Loser trying
To promote his book
Using hash tags
Hey I really don't know
Where I'm going with this
But as far as my life
That makes perfect sense
Every breath
Hey I really don't know
Where I'm going with this
Why because my life
Is going nowhere
Hardly ever sleep but I'm
Living a fucking nightmare
Facing every day
Having to hide my demons
When all I want to do
Is pray and ask God
To take them all away
Now it seems like
He stopped listening
While all their
Conversations
Inside my head
Became way more in depth
Know I'm destined for Hell
So I can't escape them

Robert Ragan 93

Even in death
Just said all that
To let you know
I'm not the person
You think I am at all
Like what the Hell
Does being possessed
Have to do
With packing my clothes
In a trash bag
I don't know
I'm just writing down
Random thoughts
About life and reality
Yeah I'm just writing down
Random thoughts
About the spirits
That control my impulses
There's blood in those visions
As long as it all belongs to me
Everything will be okay
Tell me am I too wrapped up
Inside my thoughts
Or am I just talking
Out of my head
Anyway while I'm at it
One more thing
These people say
They're your friends
Yeah they got your back
But just as long
As the problem
Is all shit talking
Let someone start swinging

94 Nothing Is Sacred

See how fast they back up
And become a spectator
Out of everyone I know
There's only one person
Who wouldn't let
Anyone fuck with me
Okay I'm gonna go now
Wish me luck in sentencing
These demons
To the prison
In the back of my mind
Oh and try to love each other
Do your best to try
And support one another
Don't ever forget
That there's always
Hope for you
It's so easy to forget
That there is still
Hope for me
Especially with my life
Steadily going nowhere

Robert Ragan 95

Read It And Weep [The Story Of Jody]

Dog while you're at work
Providing for her
And all that shit
I slide up behind her
And ask
Are you ready
For some more
Of this dick
Fuck that motherfucker
You know he don't hit it
Like I hit it
She should cuckold you
Make you watch
Just so you know
Maybe you might learn something
Oh I forgot they don't teach size
And it's not only the sex
She even loves me more
Don't worry
I don't love that whore
Jerking me off
With her engagement and wedding
Rings around her finger
What's funny about it
Is that I'm broke and
Don't have a pot to piss in
Honestly I don't know how
I do it
But you can bet your ass
I'm fucking doing it right
That sorry good for nothing
Won't work in a pie factory ass loser

96 Nothing Is Sacred

Big ol dick bigger than yours
Making your bitch's ass looser
You bitch ass loser
I'm the reason your woman
Drops you off for work in the morning
And keeps your car all day
You clock in around seven
She picks me up
About a quarter after
We usually smoke
What's left of a quarter
Picking on you
Your car filled with laughter
Hell most of the time
I end up driving that bitch
Without a lick ah license
Glad you have good insurance
Cause I drive the Hell
Out of your shit
Fuck the Hell
Out of your bitch
Even in the car
Mostly she spends the day
Driving me all over the hood
Looking for Percoset
So many times she wished
That you would take a double shift
Cause when you
Get off work that's it
You never get a hot meal
And all the leftovers are gone
If we spent the day there
Then you wonder why

Robert Ragan 97

She never wants to fuck you
When she finally
Gets tired of your begging
You find the pussy
All red and swollen
Like it got
Beat the fuck up
That's because it did
All day long
While you were at work

98 Nothing Is Sacred

High Confused With Love

Wrapped up in you
It's still cold
I find myself lost
With no direction in life
But it's okay
Because I'm going nowhere with you
Hold the smoke in
Don't let it out
Until I have
The right thing to say
Talking about your
Beauty and brilliance
Just won't cut it
No not this time
I need something sharper
Your eyes your eyes are what
Golden behind the blue
Bringing warmth to everything you see
No I have to do better than that
I don't know if I can right now
All I can say
Is my love is the truest
The words will eventually
Come in a flood
Of love and creativity
Filled with light and purity
Sorry it's so dark right now
Just please don't let my heart down
Wrapped up in you
But my soul is still freezing
Lost with no hope

Robert Ragan 99

No where to go
But it's okay
Because we're lost
With no hope
No where to go
Let's hold the smoke in
Until reality is far below us
Our love alive in the sky
Can never die
Wish we never had to come
back
Wish we never had to come down

100 Nothing Is Sacred

Cheers To The Nonexistent

Playful cheapshots with memes
I see em I see em
Think you're pushing buttons
Yeah you hit the laugh track
So you think
My feelings are hurt big time
Telling people
You feel bad about
How it all went down
Me I'm like
Feel bad about what
How did what go down
Anyway keep telling everyone
You broke my heart
Yeah it hurt for a day
But it stopped
When I realized
We both dodged bullets
Yeah we're both full of shit
But darling you are the fullest
Hey I enjoy the attention
I'm honored that breaking my heart and
Playing me for a fool
Is the highlight of your love life
You know you love me
Just a little bit
Or you would have never
Paid me a second thought
Knowing me
I just think
You're thinking about me

Robert Ragan 101

I obsess over
You obsessing over me
But you're really not
Truth is you already forgot me
I just think everything is about me
Well not everything
Just if it's negative
If it's something bad
It's got to be about me
No really am I even real

102 Nothing Is Sacred

Always You

It was you
When I was down
It was you
Who lifted me up
You've been gone
For a long time now
But you still
Give me a boost
A helping word
When your
Helping hands can't reach
You tell me
What's best for me
Behind the scenes
You don't preach
Nor do you gossip
It was you
In my heart
It was you
Who lifted me up
In my mind
It was you
Maybe I've been under a spell
Another love who put me
Through Hell
But after all that
It's you again
Everything comes back to you
It will always be you
Thanks for putting up with me

The Day You Got Rid Of Me

Oh I was so sad
It was simply a tragedy
I didn't think
I'd ever get through it
Wait I'd lost way
Better women than you
Ones I'd actually met
You were basically
An internet scammer
Posing as a artist
Sometimes a poet
Looking back
I see you weren't
Talented at either one
I just said you were
So you'd show me your pussy
The day I saw that monster
I should have got rid of you
Laughing
All the way
To the bank
Better than crying
It was a sad Friday
Money short
You were about to leave me
For the very last time
Remember there were plenty
Sounded like it hurt you
But I didn't buy it
If it hurt
You should have never said it
That goodbye cost me

104 Nothing Is Sacred

But you'll never regret it
Weren't you sort of like
A prostitute Anyway
Now that you deceived me
I think it's alright to say
Never mind these memories
All night all day believe me
 dragging you head first
The blades of

Regrets and
Consequences
Gleaming
Catatonic

Frightening Gospel

Take away the internet
I miss the oblivious days
When we didn't know
How messed up
The world really is
Wanna follow blindly
Like the days
When we didn't know
How crooked
The government really is
Oh you knew all along for years
Well I was blessed with blissful ignorance
The worst thing back then
Was Marilyn Manson's
Anti-Christ Superstar
My mom heard about it
And snapped my CD in half
It's ok I had a friend
Dub it the next day
On an unlabeled blank cassette
In my bedroom I'd
Listen to it full blast
Mom would yell and ask
You aren't listening
To Marilyn Manson are you
No mom I'd say it's Korn
Yeah I miss those days
I didn't know shit
And it was the best time of my life
All we knew about drugs
Were how they made us feel
Now I can't even get high

106 Nothing Is Sacred

Without worrying if I'm gonna
Die or just become a vegetable
Bring back the days
When I was oblivious
And knew nothing of oblivion
It all started with the internet
A hunger for knowledge
Led to the total
Corruption of my mind
I thought I did
But I didn't really want to know
I never wanted to know

Remember That

Devastating
Watching you
Pack your things
Memories return
Flood of emotions
Enough blood and tears
To fill the ocean
But you were still gone
I should have laughed
Told you
I seen it all coming
From miles away
I should have told you
To get lost
To find yourself
Somewhere
Undervalued
Unappreciated
That's the way
You made me feel
Like I was too stupid
To see through your games
I hung on your promises
All of them broken
With the way you treated me
No I don't miss you
I just try to make sure
I don't end up
With another version of you

108 Nothing Is Sacred

Forever

Really
Who did you
Think you were fooling
Behind my back
Had your knives out baby
Sad when I had
Our lives planned out
With you as my lady
Might have thought
You drove me crazy
But I got a ride back
Now I see it all
For what it was
I'll never love again
Cause look at love
And what it does
It becomes a disease
And I don't want it
It becomes a ghost
Hell yeah I was haunted
But I made it past
All those memories
Featuring you
Now all I have left
Is me
Me
I'm what matters most now
In my life
I feel so selfish

Long Ago

Do you remember
Wasting all our time
Yes yours too
What was it you promised
Said you would never
Cheat on me
Said you would never
Leave me
Well now you're gone
You're with someone else
It just couldn't be me
I just hate
That you think
You got the best of me
I knew all along
I had it all figured out
And I was never wrong
Had it all picked apart
The truth
Came to light
It was all so bright
It broke my heart
But then the pain
It all ended
I'm here now
Having went through this
You're still here now too
Do you remember
How can I ever really forget

110 Nothing Is Sacred

Defeated

Does it always
Have to be sad
Weren't we
Supposed to be in love
Wasn't I supposed
To hold your name Sacred
Love
Love
It was love
It was always so sad
Thinking of you
But only holding
Your spirit closely
It was love
It was love
Why did it
Have to be so ghostly
I wanted to know you
Inside and out
Your body
Your mind
I wanted all of you
But you and me...Us
It was always so sad
Knowing your heart
Would never beat with mine
It would never love me
The way I needed it to

Robert Ragan 111

You

It was right there
We had our world
In our hands
We had love
In our hearts
No negative energy
With you
I rose to the ceiling
With you
My fingertips were electric
Told this story so many times
I keep all the details clear
Because that night
That night
We became one
Had to be something
With you
All I wanted
Was to have something
With you
But it always
Had to be sad
Happy endings
Fairy tales
Tragedy
Then
Chaos and
Havoc
Then again
It's you

112 Nothing Is Sacred

Phantom Of The Video Call

Only truly had me
Under your spell
During our two
Eight hour video calls
Dark...
When we started talking
It was light out...
When we let each other go
The dark and the light
Both have this
Special significance here
As you had
Two different looks
The way you looked
Inside your place
In the light
And the way
You looked in the dark when
Smoking a cigarette or
Walking your big beautiful dog
Both looks...
Captured and captivated me
Not to mention
All the ways
You turned me on
Come forth witness
My mind enter
A gutter far beyond
Mere criminal behavior
Seeing you in nothing
But your bra

With your hand
Buried between your legs...
Instant Screenshot
And it's not like
I was a pervert
Taking the pics
Without your knowledge
Remember baby
You reminded me
To take them
So drunk
So high
It felt like
I was in a porno
Seeing you
Play with your pussy
On A Video Call

114 Nothing Is Sacred

That Night

That night
Captured us
We went around
In love
Like lunatics
That night
Made us different
I couch surfed
Caught some waves
In the trailer park
How many times
Have I said that
Just want you to know
When I really needed you
Never mind
I still need you
But I know
I can never have you
But your spirit
The one I connected with
That night
I hold it closely
I hold it dearly
You're so close
I have no idea
Why you can't feel me
My spirit with you
But you don't ever feel me
That night
It took apart of me
After you

Robert Ragan 115

There is nothing else
I still feel you with me
But Captured
In this reality
Without you
But no one
Can ever
Take
That night
From us

116 Nothing Is Sacred

Last 23 Minutes

Know you're not going to like this
But I'm going out with my friends
All weekend to cheat on you
But I do have like an hour to talk
Before I leave
So tell me
How Beautiful I am
How I'm the greatest artist
How I'm the greatest poet
Greatest weed dispensary worker
Of all time
Oh well there is my friend
What is she doing here early
Told her to give me an hour
To talk to you
Oh well it's not like
You really matter anyway
So what you're writing
A poetry collection about me
Trust that I've had
Far better poets than you
Write about me
Anyway this is the last
You will ever hear from me
It was not nice knowing you
Except for the times you
Sent me money in the mail
I'll miss those times but that's it
Hangs up on me...
Walks outside
Girl what took you so long

Robert Ragan 117

You actually caused me
To have to talk to that ugly loser
For an entire 23 minutes
It's ok
It's all over now
Hopefully he kills himself soon
That was the last time we ever talked
Bet the money is still the only thing
You ever miss about me

Your heart is pure evil
But I know it's made of gold
Around other people
It shines so bright
Especially when you're
Talking to him
Tell me did you get naked
For him on a video call
I'm sure you did
Anyway that was the last 23 minutes
Of our relationship
It meant nothing to you
But meant everything to me
To this day
No word from you
You're still a ghost
Just know that
Nothing Is Sacred
And with all those words
I'm shedding light
On all your darkness

118 Nothing Is Sacred

Robert Ragan 119

Vice Grips

So foolish
Very stupid
Writing about
All these women
But you did make sure
To cover the struggle
The struggle
It's all we really have isn't it
Crooked police
Arrested
Miranda rights
Try to talk to your daughter
But then Miranda fights
Keep on going son
Someday you'll get it right
Just stop talking about
All these women
I mean where are they now
You've got to let em all go
But you don't know how
Well I tell you
Writing about em all the time
Isn't going to solve anything
Come on son
You have your own life
Your own demons
Your own drug problems
Yeah you definitely covered
That part of the struggle
Didn't you
Waiting
Waiting

120 Nothing Is Sacred

Some more
Then you're still waiting
Waiting for what
Your own destruction
Digging your own grave are you
That's what you get
For waiting so patiently
The end
Nothing left of you
But memories
All the times
You got fucked up
And all the women you've fucked
That's what your life
Boils up to
Can't bring it back
And cook it
Too bad

Pick On The Weak

While I'm still up
Diving into desperation
Let's talk about you
Yeah you
Crossed that double
Didn't you
So slick
How you
Spread the word
You're just a saint
Aren't you
No I really
Think you're a snake
The words you speak
Aren't true
False criminal
Society welcomes you
With open arms
While the cold
Tries to freeze me to death
That's the difference
You could never live like this
You're just a tourist
And eventually you
Will jump ship
When the waves
Take your dignity
You've got a family
Glad you're life
Is going great
But since I'm still up
Let me tell you

122 Nothing Is Sacred

To your face
You're fake
Look at me
Up At All Times Of The Night
Talking about a fucking bozo
He already has a pointy nose
Plant that big red one
Right on top of it
Yeah man
You're a fucking clown
Are you really
Proud of yourself
Cancel culture king
Say something he doesn't like
He and his buddy
Put together a posse
And try to take away all your dreams
Would be an honorable
Thing to do
But not when
The skeletons
In your own closet
Aren't addressed
Really it sounds
Like you're
A fucking hypocrite

You Imagine It All

I've seen the dealers
Scared to death
Twelve
Gathered up
In the church parking lot
Plotting to
Serve those warrants
Fiends like me
Scattering for crumbs
Before we crawl
Back under a rock
You think you've seen
Anything like that
Well that ain't
The half of it
Man you got a cozy life
The wife the kids
You wouldn't know
How to react
To none of the things I go through
In trying to teach you
That you can't fuck with me
I'm also trying to help you grow too
See it isn't all bad
Anyway hope you have
A Happy New Year
Even fakes and snakes
Need peace in their life
Whatever you come back with
Won't come close to stopping me
I've seen way too much
To be intimidated

124 Nothing Is Sacred

By the likes of you
Especially when everything I do
Gets more likes and views
Good night
And
Good riddance

Up Your Nose And Around The Corner

In the spot
Sometimes I watched
Them cook the shit
Right in front of me
Like a hibachi restaurant
Hold on
Hold on
Goddamn
Light on the baking soda
Heavy on the cocaine
I don't even understand
Crackheads these days
Going after that shit
Like mindless zombies
Hell the first hit
Is the best
After that
You're just chasing a high
You will not
Achieve again that night
No matter who you rob
Or even if you're mother
Gives you twenty dollars
Just to get rid of your
Sorry pathetic begging ass
All of you should be
Ashamed of yourselves
Give me something
To push this pipe
I might get a back hit
Your buddy stole
His father's black onyx ring

126 Nothing Is Sacred

Got lucky on
Three for fifty Friday
And there you are
Dropping pieces in
Your shirt pocket
Every time he
Turns his head
Hell if you've just got
To have cocaine
Snort some fucking powder
As a matter of fact
Why don't you grow up
And snort and smoke meth
Like a real man
Bitch if you caught on fire
I wouldn't piss on you
To put it out
No being real
Just drink and smoke loud
Occasionally bust one down
And snort a Percoset
Now that's what the fuck
I'm talking about

Crime Of Life

Kicked to the curb
Just for being me
Didn't want to be homeless
Out in the sticks
Away from everyone
So I had to
Become one with the city
First off I found a picnic table
At the park
Sometimes I slept on top of it
Other times I got under it
Spent my days at the library
Should have been
Looking for jobs online
Instead I was studying
All my favorite writers
At the time
I was trying to get sober
Fuck that
I had to get some weed
This one time
I was helping a buddy
Haul a load of
Scrap metal and angle iron
We took it to the yard
Got the money
Then went right to the weed spot
I got some bud
Then got dropped off
Back at the library
High as Hell
That night I had a flashlight

128 Nothing Is Sacred

I shined it on the paper
So I could see
To write a new story
One all about
Being broke
Dead broke financially
Plus broken inside mentally
Once I got tired
I went and got my
Flimsy little blanket
Hidden in the woods
I went to sleep
Underneath the picnic table
Had a nightmare
That my mother
Came back from the dead
All her ashes reformed
She was skin and bones again
Her eyes were rolled back
And she kept screaming
Screaming at the bottom of her lungs
Screaming without end
Until I felt someone lightly
Kick me in the shoulder
I turned and they
Kicked me again
Only harder this time
I opened my eyes
Realized
I wasn't with my dead mother
No I was underneath the picnic table
Out in the freezing cold
With a cop yelling at me

Robert Ragan 129

Wake up wake up
Wake the fuck up
Get the fuck up
What are you doing
Sleeping under this picnic table
No one is supposed
To be in this park after hours
And look at you
Fucking living here
I said I'm sorry sir
I'm homeless and this just
Seemed like the safest
Place to be
I was hoping
He would tell me
To get the fuck outta there
But no
He had to fuck with me
Told me to empty my pockets
Right there on the table
Back then they would
Lock you the fuck up
Over possession of Marijuana
So you already know
Now I had a place to stay for awhile
Fuck I'd rather sleep
On the fucking picnic table
Rain sleet or snow
Than be locked the fuck up
In the county Hell
Had some badass brothers
In that bitch
Beating up white boys
And taking all their fucking trays

130 Nothing Is Sacred

I stayed to myself
Didn't talk to anyone
Just read a book
Thankfully I never
Got beat up for a tray
Before I got out
An older tattooed white man
Ended up in my cell
He was talking
A lot of big shit
About having ties
To the Aryan Brotherhood
I said man
They're about to fuck you up in here
You at least better shut the fuck up
About those Aryan ties
I can already tell by your tattoos
He looked at me said
Bo I ain't scared
Of a motherfucker in here
Yall pussies might let em
Bully ya'll around
But I'm gonna fight like Hell
He fault like Hell alright
Still got the Hell beat out of him
By a younger black guy too
Got Mr Aryan ties
Backed in a corner and
Lit his ass up
With hard rights and lefts
To the ribs, stomach and chest
Since he had his face
Covered with his arms

Robert Ragan 131

Before it was over
He did get in
A couple of shots to the face
One good enough
To get this guy's mouth bleeding
I told him
Man fuck all that gang shit
Just try to get along
With everyone like I do
You see they don't fuck with me
Once I peeped the scene
And got to know a few people
I got out of the books
Started talking joking and laughing
I'd be in that bitch battle rapping
Brothers talking bout
Goddamn that white boy
Talking that shit
Listen to him
Shit I'm good
Wherever I go
Hang out with
Saints and sinners
Lovers and haters
Thieves and givers
Right before I had
To go back to court
My buddy
Who I helped out
The day before I got locked up
Well he shows up on A Block
I walked up to him asked
What the fuck
Are you doing in here

132 Nothing Is Sacred

Shaking his head side to side
He said man...
You're not going to like this
I asked him
What the fuck has it got to do with me
All that scrap metal and iron
He said I stole all that shit
They got me on video
At the scrapyard cashing it all in
They wanted to know
Who was with me
I told em it was you
You son of a bitch
You didn't have to
Tell em it was me
You could have
Made up some name or something
I'm gonna tell em
I wasn't with you
When you stole the shit
Thinking about it
I said fuck they're never
Going to believe me
Motherfucker
You fucking snitched on me
We should really fight it out
Right here right now
Because of you
Now I'm gonna
Get more charges
You already know
That means more time
Anyway just stay away

From me in here
You're not my friend
If anyone asks
You don't know me
And damn sure don't
Tell anyone
I'm your co defendant
Bitch you're lucky
I don't tell
Everyone on this whole block
How you snitched on me

134 Nothing Is Sacred

Like It Is How It's Gonna Be

Put photos of her in a collage
She told her co workers
I put her in a nice college
They asked
What are you going to school for
She got this really confused look said...
I don't go to school anymore
When would I have the time
We all work here
A co worker answered
I didn't know maybe you
Started going at night
They both just needed
To shut the fuck up
If you're stupid and
Don't know what in the Hell
You're talking about
Please do the world a favor and
Just shut the fuck up
Instead of brains
I swear she has a bowl of fruit
Only not fresh fruit no
I'm talking about that plastic fruit
You know you're ass
Pulled off a grape and tried to eat one before
Don't get me wrong
I'm definitely far from a rocket scientist
The bricks have a higher IQ
But damned if this bitch won't stupid
Yeah stupid enough to fuck with me
Knowing I'd fuck her then

Robert Ragan 135

End up roasting her alive
Hey don't take any of this too seriously
I know you're ass
Doesn't literally eat grapes
Hey if it did I think
I'd like to watch that shit
Oh you know
What I mean by roasting
This is comedy not horror
I guess what I'm trying to say is
I don't have a bitch chopped up
And ready to go in the oven or do I
Wasn't I talking about
Putting my cats in the oven
Damn I better throw
That bitch out in front yard
Place trashy as Hell
Looking worse than
Fred Sandfords junk yard
You know you hear that music now
And for the record
It's IQ test not Haiku test
Could it possibly
Get any dumber than this
You ask well the answer is yes
It gets round room
Piss in the corner stupid
The dumbest shit she ever did
Was believe it when I said
I'm gonna love you and
Take care of you and
Yes I promise I'll pull out
Don't think this bashing
Is all one sided

136 Nothing Is Sacred

Her and me every night
We battle rapped and
Had ruthless roasting sessions
Talking that real shit
To the bitch and that bitch
Talked that real shit to me
Broke ass motherfucker
Want a bitch to walk around
Naked in nothing but high heels
Don't give a fuck if she falls
Through your weak ass floors
Ya bitch ass don't even have a car
I need a man who leaves
Marks on the pavement
Not skid marks in his drawers
Me I'm standing there
Clapping my hands
Stomping my foot
Like get him girl
Tell that motherfucker
Oh that's right bitch
You talking to me
That's alright remember I swore
I'd never hit you
That pussy though
I'm gonna beat it the fuck up
For all the mean shit you say to me
Baby tell me I ain't
Never gonna amount to shit
While I'm hitting it
Bitch fucked around and
Got really brutal
Comparing my dick size

Robert Ragan 137

To all the horses and goats
She was fucking
I said bitch
You wouldn't be whining
Over my little bitty dick
If your pussy wasn't blown out
Fat enough to take a monster

138 Nothing Is Sacred

Corner Rats

Why do demons always hang out in the corner
Does their horned daddy make
 them stand there when they
 misbehave
If so that snout should be
 touching the walls
There's one sitting in my corner
right now as I write this
When you're not scared watch
them cower like a disobedient dog
It sits there with smoky sulfur eyes whimpering when I yell
Turn the fuck around and stick your nose in that corner
Most would pray for it to go away
But I'm kinda having fun
Now that I've turned the tables
No thought can disturb me
So hit me with your best shot
They already felt the need to
come see me in the flesh
Red face of raw meat
Those fangs are yellow in
serious need of brushing
I tell this freak to get the fuck out of my trailer
Don't come back until you can scare me again

Truce

Shook hands
Laughed
With my enemies
Offered em
A little cash
Since I was up
Know how it feels
To be down
But I've been
Through too much
To stay down
Listen to what
I say now
I keep em
Closer than my friends
Almost State Property
In this bitch
Cause when they lay down
Those motherfuckers gonna stay down
Out here flying high
Laws are meant to be broken right
Talking about a shootout
Bitch you gonna
Get dragged out of your car
Smoking a pipe
Damn shame
Damn I'm ashamed
To even speak
On the world
I know today
One things for sure
I'm not making

140 Nothing Is Sacred

The situation any better
Breathing up all your air
Doesn't matter
Because I'm up now
Had a pocket full of cash
Now all that's left
Is a fifty dollar bill
In a soda bottle
With a ton of loose change
Fuck a bank
There's my life savings
In this bottle
Hopefully I can add to it
Week after week
Ones fives tens
They can all go
Twenties Fifties Hundreds
Any of em
Could end up in my plastic bottle
With the screw on lid
Yeah I've shook hands
With enemies
Who would smile in my face
Then take my money
And all my shit
Then I started fighting back
And we all know
How the drama
Is with me
Had to punch the motherfucker
Right in his teeth
A shot strong enough
To make his mouth bleed

Robert Ragan 141

Talk To Your Soul

A lot of yall
Are running around here
Getting big headed
Talking about you
Don't write poetry
You write checks
Yeah and them bitches
Bounce all over town
Mr Ounce to a pound
You love to hear
Your own voice
Everyone else
Frowns at the sound
And I don't give a fuck about
All the dope you sold
All the bitches you fucked
All the guns you shot
One question...
Where's all of it now
You're just as broke
And bummy as I am
Only you can't get money
Like I can
Talking about you refuse
To work a nine to five
Boy you better hope
Crime starts paying soon
Skin and bones
Looking like you barely eat
Dog how the fuck
Are you even staying alive
You little fucking Bee Gee

142 Nothing Is Sacred

I ain't got shit
Living in a trashy ass trailer and
You'd still sell your soul to be me
Yeah I heard you talking shit
He ain't gonna never make it
With that writing bullshit
He just needs to hang it up
And start hustling
On the side after work
Oh that's right
You write checks not stories
Yeah they don't tell on you
Right there at the counter
The way the plastic does
Mr Card forever declining
Even you're hair is receding
Goddam I'd be ashamed
And keep my fucking mouth shut
I damn sure wouldn't be out here
Popping shit like I was special
But oh you're a rebel
Going nowhere in your rebellion
Against brain cells and common sense
Bitch ass talking about
Pussy drugs and guns
You ain't got the money
To even keep a bitch
Or a gun to shoot the guy
She'd be fucking behind your back
Damn man
You are fucking wack
I don't know what else
To say about you

Robert Ragan 143

Know you're gonna run that trap
Yeah that mouth
Is the only trap you're running
Nasty toothless
Meth addicted whores
Yeah that's the only bitches
You're fucking
Talking about
You're out here
Living your life
To the fullest
If you had a gun
You'd have to pistol whip me
Cause your bitch ass
Can't afford bullets
Yeah the crime fiction pistol whipping king
Finally brought it to poetry
But you wouldn't know
Anything about that you
Hard-core thief and crook
That would mean reading a book
When's the last time you read one
Oh they didn't have
Dick and Jane
In the county jail
Bitch you got dicked down
Insane in the county Hell
Is that what happened
To your manhood
Said I didn't know
What else to say about you
Lines ago
Yeah you're hoping
I run out of shit to say about you

144 Nothing Is Sacred

See I look in the mirror
Then I take a look around me
Broke ass ugly motherfucker
Living in a trashy ass
Broke down trailer
With a thousand cats outside
And everyone of em
Got nine lives
Now that I said that
I probably cursed one to die
See when you take
A good look at yourself
And you see nothing
Then you can talk
Your shit to me
I can talk to your soul
Because I talked
To mine first
Admitted to the worst
Now all I can see
Is the worst in everyone else while
Most people have
Their best side at heart
Even lowdown criminals
But not you you're trash at everything
Better hope crime starts paying soon

Another Soul To Talk To

All that tough talk
Dog please stop it
This is not your notebook
Man this is real life
We're living
Do you understand me
Does what I'm saying
Make any sense
No I won't be shocked
If you stick something
Sharp inside the plug
Really you're gonna
Get locked the fuck up
You're not coming
Out of there with the drugs
The drugs
Yeah you know
A lot about those don't you
When you think about
Being tweaked out
And losing your kids
Does it haunt you
No it doesn't because
You don't care
Let that bitch
Take care of em
You got to hustle right
Always talking about brawling
Look at them arms
Boy you don't got
Enough muscles to fight
Motherfucker you knew better

146 Nothing Is Sacred

Than to come around me
Talking all that bullshit
You're lucky there's
No one else around
I would have
Made them laugh at you
Talking about you were
Involved in a drive by shooting
Yeah bitch you were
Crying in the backseat
Shall I go on
I love to expose
These so called criminals
All out of control
Say the word
And I'll say your name
Doesn't have to be subliminal
When I talk to your soul
Bitch you sold it
For a cheap chain
And a gram of ice
Sad but the only thing
Shining was the dope
No I said you're
A fucking loser
And I'm just reminding you
That you have no hope
Damn I could go on forever
I just want to know
What the fuck
Do you have to say about me
Just stop it
With all the tough talk dog please

Robert Ragan 147

I call you dog cause I wanna
See you standing tall
But man right now
You might as well
Be down on your knees
Begging praying
Sucking dick
Man you need to
Get back on your feet quick
So put the notebook away
Remember this is real life

148 Nothing Is Sacred

Talking To My Own Soul

Honestly I'm not that good
Some would say
I'm not good at all
Others would say
My writing is straight trash
I know these things
Because I have
Grapes coming out
Of my ears
Stay tuned to the vine
They turned away from the vibe
Anyway so I suck at writing
Crime fiction and poetry
But when it comes
To actual crime and poverty
I should go down in history
As one of the greatest of all time
Petty crimes of course
Well some bigger than others
So let's just say I was a role player
No that sounds too close to my sex life
Let's just say I was a dominant force coming
Off the park bench
But when it comes to poverty
I'm the Michael Fucking Jordan
Of poverty baby
Fuck the jump man
Nike needs new shoes
With a logo of me
Digging through a trashcan for food
Yeah that's how it used to be

Robert Ragan 149

Now I have a job thank God
So at least I get to eat once in awhile
If I lose that I'll be back in the dumpsters
Most people would see
The trailer that I live in
And choose to be homeless
Holes in the floors from all the leaks
Holes in the walls from acting like a bitch
Plus I have like a billion cats
So you already know
Everything else is fucked up
Despite being ugly as fuck
I used to do surprisingly well
With the ladies at times
Now I'm scared to talk to a woman
Really I want to tell em I'm homeless
But lucky enough to have a job
No matter what happens
They can't ever come over here
Not even just to pick me up
Let's just say my yard well my junkyard
Is in desperate need...well we're all
Needy around here
Bedbugs started all this
They destroyed my life
Now they're gone
And the roaches are here
Trying to get what's left
Man it's hard being this real damn
Looks like I'm never getting another date
For the rest of my fucking life
Which is probably a good thing
Any woman willing to overlook
All of this well she's probably

150 Nothing Is Sacred

Gonna have a whole lotta shit
She wants me to overlook
And if you know me
I don't overlook anything
Why you think I call myself out
I mean I will overlook some things
But baby it better be grip tight
That kind where you can't get right
Good enough to get you in a fist fight
But no woman worth having
Would ever sleep
On the kitchen floor with me
 Hell no
Come home from work
Open the refrigerator
And find a fucking dildo
Me searches frantically
I don't give a fuck about that
But where the fuck are my pills ho
I care about you I guess
But I'll kill you over my
Motherfucking pills though
Just let me know before I leave
And I'll give you a couple
But whatever you do
Don't go in my stash
Come home and kick your fucking ass
No I don't condone violence against women
Unless it's consensual
With whips chains choking and such
Have your ass dead
Wrapped in whips and chains
After I choke you way too hard

Robert Ragan 151

A little bit too much
Come on you know how I am
If I didn't love you ladies
I wouldn't give you the heads up
On my real life and tell you
How big of a fucking loser I am
No I'd lie
And waste your time
Get you over here
And try to fuck you
In this monstrosity
I call a trailer
No I'd rather tell you I'm homeless
Tell you to meet me at park bench
Don't you know it gets crazy after dark bitch
Feel like I'm on my
R.E.M Losing My Religion shit again
Oh No I've definitely said too much this time
Even all the sorry good for nothing bitches
 Won't have anything to do with me
After reading this
Damn I am literally going to be single
For the rest of my life
And it's alright
Now on another suicide note
Some of you will probably think
I'm glamorizing poverty
You know all the shit and piss
See me laying on the floor
Starving to death
Like...
You know you want to live like this
Cops kick in the fucking door
They're like we ain't searching this bitch

152 Nothing Is Sacred

Let him keep the dope he needs it
But tell the Captain we need
To have this trailer condemned
Yeah baby that's the type of life
 I'm living
Anyway I look at these pieces
Sort of life like they're
Battle rap bars
And talking to my own soul right here
I 3-0ed myself with one fucking round
Gotta a water leak
Need to go
Turn it on
At the road
Stick my head
In the tub and drown
My life is so fucking tragic
I need to wear
Nothing but a blindfold drunk
And go play in traffic
Throw away my phone
Walk somewhere on foot
Far far away from the road
Then cut my little
Bitchmade wrists
No I said stick a gun to my temple
All demons evacuate
My life and the poem
Ends like this

I Can't Be Friends With You Anymore

No it's not that serious
I'm just trying to figure out
How to get out of this jam
It has to be resolved
And for now
I can't be friends with you anymore
Let's just say
I'm catching feelings again
How could I not
When I talk to you every day
Honestly we're perfect as only friends
But I'm letting memories
Get in the way
Black stockings
On your perfect legs
The welts were covered in skulls
You made everything so hot
You could have took my soul
And how could I forget the day
You got over my knee
Then told me to spank you
I was going light
Didn't want to hit you too hard
Then you told me
That's what you wanted
So I left deep red handprints
On your firm little ass
Plus my own hand was stinging
I'll never forget what I saw
When you got up
My pants were drenched
From the knee

154 Nothing Is Sacred

All the way up to the thigh
It made me want you so bad
Fuck why did this all of a sudden
Pop back into my head
In HD full color
You're the only person
I can trust
The only one
Who could possibly
Talk me down off the ledge
Now I don't think
I can be friends with you anymore
No as a friend you're really
All I've got
So I don't want that
It's just hard
When I want more
When deep down
I want you back
But you know better
So when I ruined
What I had with you
I burned that bridge forever
Now after all these years
We've found a way to cross over
Becoming the best of friends
Can't help what
My mind flashes back to
Fuck you were so hot
You know what damn you
I don't want to be your friend anymore
Got me smiling
Literally shaking my fucking head

Robert Ragan 155

You'll never know
How proud I am of you
The dark I face
You conquered
And found the light again
You don't need any negative energy
In your presence
To keep it dim
So it's best
That we not be friends anymore
You're light is
Shining so bright
Yet you're still
Trying to save
A lost soul
From love past
Damn I have tons of stories
When it comes to women
True to life
Out of body experiences
But nothing beats the one
About the day
I got out of prison for the second time
On the other side of the gate
In that pink dress
You were all mine
The best
Never met anyone
So real
We have a ton of stories
Between us
Funny how
The best lover
I ever had

156 Nothing Is Sacred

Turned out to be
The best friend
I ever had too
Just wanted to tell you
All of this
Oh and I love you

Pray For It All To Stop

I have to sleep with the light on now
If I ever sleep at all
Now the only
Dark I'm blessed with
Is the same dark
I've lived my life
Cursed by
Sometimes it feels like
I'm in one of those movies
You know the ones
Where someone is
Losing their mind
Only I'm going further
Broken completely insane
But there's no film crew
When it all ends
Will anyone tell my story
Live by the drugs
Die by the drugs
So many visions of cuts
Severed digits
Please be no blood
Please don't let it be gory
Let me be
In and out of consciousness
Then just fade away forever
Even if it's meant to burn
Hopefully my soul
Remembers none of this
I have to sleep with the light on now
My blood is on the line
Slowly tiny tube mouth glow

158 Nothing Is Sacred

May all of you smile for the camera
That's not really there
Why can't these late nights be romantic
A touch
A talk on the phone
We'll maybe I'm just meant to be alone
This love of mine so deep
But how true can love be
When love always has to be in control
So my love isn't so deep
Truly I can't love any woman
Unless she gives her life over
And bows down before me
But no one wants to take this pledge
Give up standing on solid ground
To truly live life on the edge
The edge of insanity
And I'm slipping
I fell but I'm hanging on
But there's no love there
To pull me up
Fuck love
Cram it up the asses
Of all those who hurt me
Really I understand
They're still blessed
To sleep with the light off
It's on all night at my place
But it's always
Pitch black in my mind
Tons of Boogie Men
Not so big
But they're really bad

Robert Ragan 159

Hurry up tiny tube mouth glow brighter
The imaginary cameras on
And all the bloods on the line
They're just one thing out of a million
Bet the sight of a brand new razorblade
Would make me cringe just as much
Fuck reality
I would cram it up my ass
But as you can see
I'm pretty close to losing touch
Mind like mine
I'm not losing much
Just a ton of bad memories
And stories I wanted
To share with everyone
When I'm gone for good
Will anyone tell my story
How I fought with the letters
Until they caused me
To destroy everything
Including myself

160 Nothing Is Sacred

Owe Me Well Just Blow Me

You should know by now
You can't say shit
In this haunted little small town
Without it getting right back to me
I hear your doing a lot of talking about me
But until right now I haven't really
Had shit to say about you
I mean come on you know
How I talk to souls
You know how
I talk to my own
Now take this journey with me
Because I'm about to talk about yours
Where the fuck
Is my money at
Remember you came to me
Needed the money
To buy some weight
Said if I'd help you
That you would make it
Well worth my while
Well motherfucker
I haven't seen you ever since
Running around asking everyone
If I'm mad at you
Tell me what do you really think
With me you know it's the principle
More than the money
So you can keep it
I have a job
I'll make that money back

Robert Ragan 161

But I won't ever pay
To have the bridge you burned rebuilt
There's nothing you can ever do
To make it up to me
Or earn my forgiveness
Just remember when
You're out there
Struggling and desperate
Everyone you turn to says No
Just remember I
Would have helped you if I had it
None of you surprise me
With your dishonor or
dishonesty
None of you have
A moral code these days
And it shows
I mean you can be all fuck the law
Fuck the system
You can turn your back on people
But there has to be someone
Who you won't cross once
Yet alone double cross
If not eventually I promise you
There will come a time
When you've literally burned every bridge
When that time comes
You're gonna have to swallow your pride
No excuse me
Crush it down and snort it then
Either way that pride
Is gonna take a little lashing
I know you don't believe me
Like fuck this stupid motherfucker

162 Nothing Is Sacred

But one day I swear you'll see
Hopefully you wise up before then
And do a whole lotta growing up
Oh and by the way
I am still done with you
But as far as this
Just know that I talked to your soul very lightly
Now I'm gonna take this loss
So shut the fuck up about me
You know longer know me
Or have any reason at all
To even mention my name

What Will You Say To My Soul

Look at this little bastard
Saying he's gonna
Talk to my soul
Bitch better get a whole team
To write for me
Ya'll still won't
Come up with shit
If I was ya'll
I'd study all
My love poetry
Figure out
Things to say
About that
No I might
Call me a bitch
For even writing the shit
No I'd talk about that rejection
I'd say it's over for me
In the world of publishing
Yeah there's a ton of wounds
A ton of weaknesses
That you could all exploit
Only you don't think
The way that I do
Your pens don't write the same
Your thumbs don't type the same
Pretty much you're all lame
You should put together an anthology
And invite all your friends to submit
Call it...Poetry To Put Your Ass To Sleep
And I mean asses literally
All them butts in bed

164 Nothing Is Sacred

Ain't no poops taking
On your watch
No seriously you should call it
Poetry To Put You To Sleep
Resting your heads on soft pillows
All of you are sheep
Coming off as corny
In your desperate attempts
To look dark and edgy
Anyway take my advice
Put together a team
Of writers that hate me
And tell em to
Put their pens to work
Let's see what
You little motherfuckers
Come up with
I'm sure I'll get a laugh
Seeing ya'll try
To switch up my style
And use it against me
Oh you're going
In another direction
My bridge
Was a bad one to burn
Yeah you can go in another direction
But you're headed nowhere
No matter where you turn
When are you gonna learn
That I can't be fucked with
Until you learn
Just go suck a dick and
Get the fuck outta here

Robert Ragan 165

Took This Over

Alone
Just me
No blood
No acquaintance
Coming
Hope there's
No other visitors
Tonight
Oh here he goes
Saying there's something
Evil inside his head
No there's just a brain
Inside of his head
And it's stupid
He's not haunted
It's just mental illness
Thought he'd rather talk
About the people
Who hate him
And the large penis
They can all suck
Maybe talk about the world
And how we're all fucked
Really no one hates him
Actually hardly no one
Even thinks about him
It's this war he's imagined
One where he's losing every battle
He can't even win in his own imagination
No one to talk to
No blood
No acquaintance

166 Nothing Is Sacred

Alone
Hoping no visitors
Come tonight
Dumbest shit
I ever heard
But he believes it
Sometimes I think
I'm the voice
Maybe I'm
The evil spirit
Telling you
That he's crazy
I don't want you
To believe I'm
Even true
I don't want him
To believe it either
You wouldn't believe this
But actually I'm not evil
I've just got his back
Head off full of
Mixed up thoughts
I keep him in check
Calm and scared
But beware because
I could create a monster
Pressure to act
On intrusive thoughts
Could result in something
Disastrous
He lives on the edge
In a place where
It's always raining

Robert Ragan 167

It represents his sanity
He's slipping barely hanging on

168 Nothing Is Sacred

In Spirit

Might not be there
In front of your eyes
But you best believe
I'm with you
My spirit enjoys your company
It all started with an instant message
But the moment I laid eyes on you
Something inside me changed
I've been with you ever since
I was with you
When you ghosted me
I was with you
When you wouldn't even
Talk to me
So what we weren't meant to be
Lovers but aren't you the one who told me
Friends can be soulmates
Can you feel it
When I obsess over you
I know you don't believe in God
But I still pray for you
Might not be there in the flesh
But I am always with you
Sometimes we meet again in my dreams
We are lovers and soulmates
Either that or you are plotting to kill me

What Happens Once It's Over

Bad thoughts
Eating at my brain
No literally they have fangs
They are really eating my brain
Inside the home of the skull
The visions are vivid and terrifying
Like why can't I have intrusive thoughts
About tying my shoes
Why is someone always dying
Why cause I know I got em laced tight
If my own mind doesn't drive me mad
Well this place might
Can't eat
Can't sleep
Can't think
But my mind
Is running scared
Up shit creek
In a staring contest
In the mirror
Can't blink
I've got to see
Inside my soul
To make it
Out of my head alive
Intrusive thoughts like
I can't take care
Of all these animals
But if I give em up
Some of em will end up dead
So why don't we all
Just die together
170 Nothing Is Sacred

Of course me included
When it comes down to it
I'm the only one
I could ever hurt
And if I do
Someone please
Take care of my babies
Yes Inside the home of the brain
The images are enough
To make you cry
If not that
They'll make you
Scream in terror
Bad thoughts are eating my brain alive
I can't function
I can't exist
I can't deal with this
I can't miss
Blood hides in us all
Can't see
Red has me blinded
Blood hides in us all
Ocd intrusive thoughts
Wants me to go
On a mission to find it

It Is What It Ain't

Sick cat
I hope she'll be alright
Already have too many
But not one of them
Is unwanted
I mean obviously
I didn't want this many cats
But it's what I ended up with
I know I could easily
Have em dropped off
At a shelter or even
Have animal control
Come pick them up
The thing is these cats
Are used to me and
I don't want them
To end up in a strange place
Like what happened
To the guy who
Brought food and
Held and petted us
Thinking of them feeling abandoned
Nearly brings me to tears
Of course it's stressful and irritating
Is that why OCD intrusive thoughts
Make me picture killing them
Got news for the evil spirits
Named after letters
Disguised as a mental illness
See I'll kill myself and
Leave you motherfuckers homeless
Before I ever do anything

172 Nothing Is Sacred

To harm one of my animals
You bitches will have to find
Someone else to take over
I know it won't be a problem
Just know it won't be a problem
For me to choose these cats
Over myself
I mean I do it all the time
I could have a nicer place
I could probably date again
And not feel pathetic
Like I'm the crazy cat man
In the end though
Why would I abandon them
So I can find a woman
To ultimately abandon me
Vulgar and immature to say
But you can't always pick
The pussy you love best
Sorry just had to say that
I promise someone else
Would have the same thought
Damn I just want
My white kitten
With the patch of black
On its head to be okay
If it's her time to go
Then it's just going to be
A sad time for me
I should be used
To all the sad times
They last forever it seems
While the moments

Robert Ragan 173

Filled with happiness
Have leaks allowing
It all to run out too quickly
The kitten that was such a pig
Now won't eat and is starting
To look sickly
At least I know
I never did anything
But love them
And try to be good to them
Even when I hated myself
With a fucking passion
Even when these stupid demons
Wanted me to hurt them
Reminder remember the news
I'd intentionally overdose and
Die passed out on the floor
Before I ever did anything
To hurt one of them
As a matter of fact
That's just the way
I want to go
Don't really want to hurt myself
But if I die
Just let me pass out and go
Without anyone knowing
Or even finding me
Dying is the only way
I'd ever let those cats starve
So fuck it let em feed on me
Until I'm discovered
Maybe that way
They'll always know
I stuck it out with them

174 Nothing Is Sacred

Until the very end
When I possibly couldn't
Any longer
Women I fell in love with
I tried to stick it out with them
Until the very end
They appreciated it dearly
When they didn't want it to end
But when they were done with me
My not wanting it to end
Well they didn't give a fuck about that
Anyway please God
Let my kitten
Get through this sickness
And be okay please

The Truth About Lies

We both drowned
In the tears of wrong
Sacrificing everything epic
Between us
The night we met
The dark played match maker
You were made to hurt me
Murdering everything special
That we ever had
With your lies and mind games
Your lipstick messages
Left in shards on the bathroom floor
Closing my fist tightly
I mixed my blood
With those fragments of words
You destroyed everything
That we ever had between us
With your mind games and lies
Sad but the only power
You ever had over me
Was between your legs
But at the same time I did really love you
Thought you had the moon in a noose
Even if I knew you were wrong
I still defended you rotten tooth and rusted nail
So fuck you
These other guys
Take you on nice vacations
But you know
I take you places
That they never could
With words that make you feel ways

176 Nothing Is Sacred

That they never could
Like you were really loved
That used to mean
More to you than money
You smiled so big the day you saw me
Riding on the passenger side
Of some drunks car I was using for a ride
Trying to holler at you
You and me though
We're not like most people
We see the world in words and colors
We over analyze and pick everything apart
We both lied and played mind games
You should have fucking known
You could never pull that shit on me
But you did without a second thought
Suddenly our world of colors and words
Was a world of the war between us
You know I hate you right
Still doesn't stop me
From dropping by once in awhile
At first you always tell me to leave
That if he comes home from work early
He'll kill us both
I pull out my knife and tell you
I'll cut out his Adam's apple
And make Eve eat it
Like the snake that I am
You start an argument
About the forbidden fruit
Saying it never said it was an apple
I say I don't care what you think about it
It's gonna always be an apple to me

Robert Ragan 177

Realizing I over talked you
Next you start talking about your man
He's diesel and tough
So you end up telling me that
He would make me
Eat my own knife
That's the shit that makes me crazy
The fact that you think he's so much better than me.
Yeah that's the shit that makes me crazy
Creep up on him in the dark with a gun crazy
Don't say a word just pull the trigger crazy
That's how you sacrificed
Everything epic Between us
It's how you set fire and burned away
Everything special that we ever had
Sure you tell me to leave
Yeah you say he'll kill me
But it's worth the risk
When you break down and
Use your greatest power over me
I'd walk in the Lions Den
For the scraps they left of you
Together we reached other realms
High and filled with animal lust
There was no one we could trust
The last time he worked out of town
The Night we spent together haunts me
Tangled together we were snakes making love
Blazed drunk pilled out
We were flipping the channels
Back and forth between
A horror movie and music videos
Next thing I know I was soaring through water
You were by my side

178 Nothing Is Sacred

Then all the water turned to blood
Came back to my senses
You were so beautiful in that blur
Trashy yet so classy
One arm completely sleeved with tattoos
Pills were the only times
You should have ever
Gave me the blues
Yeah I know that was corny as a motherfucker
Anyway you went on your own trip that night
Talking about your life being
A computer program
You'd been having that thought
A lot lately but you couldn't tell him
How much better is he than me
When you can't even
Talk to him about the things bothering you
By the way why is it that people
Feel the need to share
All their dirt with me
Hell no I don't want to know
Where you hid the body
I don't give a fuck about
The demon inside you
I'll just tell you
That you better keep that bastard in check
Trust me I've got my own to deal with
Anyway back to you
Yeah that night was epic
The dark outside was special
Remember how we first got together
After all our visions
After all those images

Robert Ragan 179

We ended up tangled again
Cum shot with the venom
As a masked killer
Chops off someone's head
With a hatchet on screen
Show you how I make a ratchet scream
When it was over
There we were cuddling and
Watching music videos
Before we finally fell asleep
Old sleep paralysis hag
Tells the shadows
We've finally got them
Asleep in the same bed again
You know we were meant for each other
No we were made for each other
That's why it haunts me
That you were really made to hurt me

180 Nothing Is Sacred

What Love Is

You used to say
I love you
But how
I mean seriously
Do you even know
How to love
Come on
You don't even know
What love is
For awhile I admit
You put all your heart
Into trying to convince me
That your love was true
Only it seemed so real
When the truth proved
Your colors were never true
Down deep I saw uncertainty
Digging deeper I saw hatred
I saw that love was never you
Oh I forgot more than anything
I saw a whole lotta fear
Remember less is everything
To do this day
You still go around
And tell people
How much you used to love me
Basically you been around
But I was that one true love
No basically you've been around
But I'm the one you love the most
That makes me the fucking sucker right

Robert Ragan 181

So stop telling people
How much you used to love me
If I was that one true love
You would have stopped
Getting around after me
Don't even mention my name
But if you do
Don't bring up love
In the same sentence
I mean seriously
Do you even know how to love
Come on
You don't know what love is
While I'm talking about you
I hate it but I always
Have to address the greaseballs
That come between us
All these dominants and narcissists
Think they don't have to
Assassinate my character because
I'm the good guy
The nice guy
They don't know that I'm just
Sitting back observing everything
A voice telling me
To fight back against all their bullshit
Every one of em are pathetic
I give to you
They steal from you
So fucking pathetic
I hold you close
Try to keep you safe
While they hit you
They ignore what you say

182 Nothing Is Sacred

I sit down and listen closely
But I'm the one who is fucking pathetic
Because with these guys
You know how to love them
You know exactly what love is
My love for you is the only true love
I know how to love you
I know what love is
I feel it on another level
I don't know what else to say
I've said all this a billion times
I've written about us even more
Hanging out high with my friends
Stressing them because
All I talk about is you
I have so much to say
But for now I'm gonna try to stop
Talking and writing about you
My damsel beyond distressed
Knew love in other arms
But couldn't figure it out with me
It's simple you just never really loved me
The end

The End Of Us

But really there never was an US
I pressured you early on
To say you love me
Because in the first couple of days
I said I love you
The only thing is
I really meant it
But you never did not once
Anyway this had to be
The worst weekend ever
After a stressful week
Of not hearing from you
Friday night you call
And the first thing you said
Was..." You're not going to like this babe, but I'm going out
tonight and tomorrow night "
Normally I would have been
Terrified of you cheating on me
But this time
It just hurt that you
Took the weekend away from me too
You took every bit of time
That I had with you
Yet you said you love me
No you don't
But I love you
And that's why it hurt
To have you throw me away
That's basically what you did
So I ended this
Said you would never
Get the chance

184 Nothing Is Sacred

To hurt me ever again
Come daylight Saturday
I was heartbroken
As soon as my eyes opened
I couldn't face the day
Knowing you'd be
Gone that night too
So I guess I didn't
Really want to end
Things with you
But it was too late
And Sorry Definitely
Wouldn't work this time
So I put myself back to sleep
With pills and alcohol
Slept woke up slept woke up
The last time you actually messaged
You said if I really want out so bad
You'd go on and let this go
But if not then we could try again
You said you'd call me
Sunday night when
You got off work
I passed back out with hope
Woke up today
Made it through it somehow
But tonight...
Well you didn't call me
When you got off work
I waited
When I wanted to say fuck it
I waited some more
Then finally I said

Robert Ragan 185

You know what fuck this
And sent you a message
Saying I wanted
To go through with the break up
Not because I don't love you
No because you don't love me
You never did
That's why it was so easy
To take all your time
Away From Me
A couple hours go by
And then I realized
That you're planning
One last thing
To try an emotionally cripple me
The woman traumatized
By being Ghosted
Is gonna ghost me
So in the end
I didn't even get
To break up with you
You lied to me
Probably cheated
And on top of that
You ended the relationship
Well you ended the relationship
Long ago
I know I had trust issues
And made accusations
But so would anyone else
After being pushed away
Despite my flaws
You know I loved you
And tried to show it

186 Nothing Is Sacred

In every way I knew how
It all goes to show
In the very end
You destroyed me
And yet I ended this
By trying to be giving
One last time
You said you'd call me
Tonight when you got off work
Because you wanted
To end this
By lying to me
One last time
No wait that wasn't enough
You lied to me
And you ghosted me
Right now
Sadness
Has sharpened its claws
I loved you so much
So fucking much
And all you did
Was play mind games
Ones that I
Could never win
Being i loved you so much
So fucking much
And all you did
Was hurt me
Hurt me and threw me away
So for the rest of my life
I'll always say that ultimately
You hated me

Robert Ragan 187

Hate was all you showed
No bracelet
No book cover
Still the book
Is all about you
And how you hurt me
How I loved you
And how you hated me
Sums it all up perfectly
So goodbye Beautiful
I still love you baby
Just wish you
Could have really
Loved me back

188 Nothing Is Sacred

Start Something Real With You

We talk for hours
We talk the night away
I've done all that before but
With you it's something more
Like the way you laid claim on me
When I say it out loud
Your title is everything
A Sacred Name was meant to be
Damn right now I feel so silly
But you have my spirits on cloud million
You know me so well already
So don't let my past scare you away
Nothing can stop
What I feel for you
Baby we aren't impossible
So all I want is to
Start something real with you
Like always
People think I'm crazy
Or either desperate as Hell
And like always I worry about
What they think
Still you know I'm not going to stop
If you're a mistake
I'm gonna make it
Anyway as far as those
Who think I'm crazy and
I should date someone near by
Well look at my options
All the good women
Around my way

Robert Ragan 189

Are either taken
Trying to find themselves or
They're too traumatized to date again
After being with some of these redneck thugs
Besides this isn't impossible
I'm determined and
I will make this happen
Gonna see you and the first thing
I'm gonna do is drop everything
And put my arms around you
We're gonna take pics together
Everyone will know
Because we're sharing them
From the start you've never
Kept me a secret because you're
Not ashamed of me
When I say it out loud
I think how your title
Is everything a Sacred Name
Was supposed to be
Now nothing can stop what I feel for you
So when it's time for me to leave
It can't be the end of us
No just the beginning
Because nothing can stop
What I feel for you
With all my heart I promise
All I want is to
Start Something Real With You

190 Nothing Is Sacred

Don't Nobody Care

We're at the end of this story
Our lives nothing but subplots
In the bigger picture
Everything going on
Between you and the
Love of your life
It all seems epic
Life changing to you
While the rest of us
Barely even care
Too busy living our own stories
Like me I love someone
Yeah someone who will
Never love me back
So I just go with the flow
The flow being
A steady stream of bullshit
Like I owe the plug
Three hundred dollars
And he's gonna have my head
If I don't pay him back
By the end of the month
Yeah it's some crucial shit
But trust me no one else gives a fuck
You can say you do
Oh yes it's so easy
To say you do
Oh yeah I completely understand
It's so easy to say you do
But motherfucker do you even understand
The slightest bit

Robert Ragan 191

I know you got your own thing going on
Like your Food Lion MVP card
Didn't save you shit
On groceries this week
They can say they do all day
Just to try to make themselves look good
But who really has your back
When a lame motherfucker
Tries to call you out on some slick shit
If you have one person ready to ride poetically
Then you are truly blessed
Talking about love
Well if you have a woman
More concerned about you
Than your money
Well you better hold her close
Make her feel that you love her
And hold her sacred in your heart
Because these days ones like her
Don't come around often
Remember don't Nobody care about
What you're going through
Mostly everyone is only worried
About their own drama
In the overall scheme of things
None of our lives amount to shit

192 Nothing Is Sacred

Anything Goes

Even as a thief
I had codes
Things I just
Wouldn't do
I'm trying hard
To do the right things
Work for everything I get
But if life ever
Pushes me back
To the way I used to be
I'm gonna turn it all the way up
Fuck having a code
Not when there's no honor
Amongst my kind
I'll fuck around
Steal your eye glasses
Break em
Throw em beside the road
Now you can really tell everyone
You got robbed blind
I know I know
That was lame as fuck
I'm just trying
To give you all an example
Of how fucking ruthless
I'm gonna be
If life ever pushes me back
To being the old me
While I'm at it
Might as well introduce
Firearms to the game

Robert Ragan 193

You don't have to be sneaky
Waiting for someone to leave home
With a pistol I could
Knock on the door
Come in and make myself at home
Better yet I could
Have you gladly give me
Anything I want
Yeah most people fantasize
About winning the lottery
While my mentally unstable ass
Imagines committing armed robberies
Keep pushing life
Life just keeps on pushing me back
To the old me
To the way I used to be
Only this time
There's no codes to follow
Could make it a blood trail

194 Nothing Is Sacred

Warned You

Oh the web i weave
Do the right thing
Maybe do the wrong thing
But I make them all believe
I've instigated fights
I've stopped fights
Talk both sides through it
I've been in the places they imagined
Won and lost in those places
Stories from backroads hoods
Ya'll want to go to war with me
So bad your wives can taste it
All so superior
So sad when your
Lives are wasted
They want to put me down
But in case they missed it
I'm already down
I've been down
For along time
I was told countless times
That I would never
Amount to shit
So I kept doing what I love
Couldn't let the shallow
Make me quit
Now there's no time to argue
Over things that aren't real
Not when I owe the dope man
A lot of cash
And there's a price on my head

Over this bad deal
All you motherfuckers
Need to get real
Now when you talk shit
I just ignore it
Even though I know all about it
None of you are capable
Of becoming real
Now when you talk junk
I say Even though you hate me
I hope you have a blessed day
Then put a hex on em
Because I woke up
On the wrong side
Of the floor the next day
Fuck all of you who hate me for no reason

196 Nothing Is Sacred

All Night Conversation

Need to sleep
But I'm up late
Lost in you
I've already told you
I need to go
I keep letting you talk
Because I really don't want to go
In the morning
You'll be safe and sound in bed
I'll be up contemplating calling out of work
But I can't
So don't be mad
If I wake you up
With a good morning text
I'll be texting you at break at lunch
Any free time I get in between
For now tomorrow doesn't matter
Not when I'm getting to know you
I've got so much love in my heart
I hope we keep talking and
I eventually get to show you
I want to write things
That make you laugh
Things that make you feel loved
I want to write things
That make you feel empowered
Things that you can carry with you
Even if you decide I'm not what you want
I can't do that because I knew right away
That you're exactly what I want
You are everything I want

Robert Ragan 197

So let's light the dark
Let's free our hearts
Gonna wish I'd slept
In the morning
But this is a great place
For us to start

198 Nothing Is Sacred

After The Divorce

That is best picture
Of you I ever seen
No just kidding
It's the ugliest damn picture
I might have ever seen in my life
I've seen a lot
After all you are my ex wife
Anyway whoever took that picture
Should have their hands cut off
After that someone should use em
To slap em up side the damn head
Baby that's how damn ugly
You are in that picture
Sorry honey
After seeing your true colors
In divorce court
I really just think that
You're ugly as shit
No I won't tell anyone
How your parents had to tie a
Porkchop around your neck
To get the dog to play with you
No I won't tell anyone
How they had
To pay someone
To take you to the prom
Really I feel cheated
Hell I married you
And didn't get the first piece
Of porkchops
Baby with makeup on

Robert Ragan 199

You look like a clown
But with your makeup off
You look like a horses asshole
Not to mention
I can never eat seafood again
Ever since the first time
You took your panties off
So yeah darling that's one
Ugly ass picture of you
Even if you felt cute
Don't hesitate delete
That ugly motherfucker right now
You always look like
A horses asshole in the face
But in that pic
Sweetie you look like
A horse's asshole
With shit coming out of it.
Sorry I know I'm being really mean
But hey I can be this mean
Because I already know
That I ain't shit
I already know any woman
Worth a damn
Wouldn't have anything to do
With a stupid
Ugly ass loser like me
Taking pictures looking like
The Toxic Avenger wearing a toupee
Now that I think about it
Honey we should reconsider
This whole divorce thing
Hell it looks like no one else
Will have either one of us

200 Nothing Is Sacred

So we might as well be together
No I'm just kidding
I'd rather cut my dick off
Put it on a bun and
Pretend it's a sausage dog
Than ever stick it in you again
Yes babydoll I'm well aware
That you think it's the
Littlest tiniest peter
You ever seen
Way to little and tiny
To try worming it's way
Inside a mammoth vagina like yours
Anyway I'll talk to you later
By the way
I'm not really married
I've never been married in my life
If I had
Along with ex girlfriends
I'd have an ex wife
I've been engaged twice
More like enraged really

Slow Down Speed Up

As bad as I need it
I'm still running
From the money
The electric company
Don't give a fuck
If I need mental health days
Sleeping dreaming all day
After another all nighter
As broke as I am
I'm still running
From the money
Seeing the wreck
I live in
Rotting to its core
I think if
Life is what you make it
Then I've made
A fucking disaster out of mine
Running from the money
Ultimately I'm running out of time
Every day it's go to Hell
Come back home
Wait what do you do
When home is another
Version of Hell
At least at home
I can sit amongst the ruins
And be the failure
I was always meant to be
Yeah at least I can cry at home
Facing the day on someone else's time
I have to strive for way more

202 Nothing Is Sacred

Than I'm actually capable of
All while holding back tears
Even the good days at work
Are destroyed when
I come home
As bad as I need it
As broke as I am
I keep running...hiding
Like the money is out to get me
I've got to bring back the old me
The one dead set out to get the money
That guy had a new short story
To write every day of the week
Guess I'm not only running from the money
Looks like I'm also running
From my goals and all my passion for art
I just want to run away from life
Run out of breath
Run from all the reasons to stay
Run even further away
From all the reasons
To keep going on with life

Robert Ragan 203

I Love you You Hate Me

Don't you dare romanticize
How much we went through
I mean how much I went through
After all I was the one burning in Hell
Trying to convince you
Darling it's only a
Urinary Trac infection
I promise you
I don't have any kind
Of STD's
That would take sex right
If so well I'm good
Haven't had any what you call it
Since it had me
Anyway you trying
To get freaky or what
Don't you dare glamorize the struggle
Remember that time
I was almost broke and
You had the nerve to order a combo
I had it all worked out
Even asked if you had a problem
Eating off the dollar menu
You said no
Then got up there talking bout
Let me get a number ten
With a large coke
Excuse me miss but
I was planning to get
Water cups to steal Sprite
There I was sitting at the table
Mean mugging with a measly little cheeseburger

204 Nothing Is Sacred

While you sat there eating like a queen
Talking bout how your last boyfriend
Took you to all these fancy restaurants
I said Well stop all your crazy shit
And maybe he'll take you back
Don't ever let me hear
How bad you've got it
I'm the only one
Who ever struggled
In this relationship
Hey I do the best I can
But since I don't have
A pocket full of money
To you I'm not a real man
Well baby sorry to tell you
But I don't give a fuck
What you think

You Wouldn't Be Proud

Oh look mom
I'm being
Dark edgy and crazy
They say I say things
That most people won't say
Probably because those people
Have pride and dignity
Most likely because
They have more sense
Than to say things like that
That's the name of game though
Bleed to try to make them understand
Bleed even when the word
Blood makes you cringe
Bleed some more
Just to see the vampires
Spit it back in your face
Your energy
Nothing but a feast
Your soul lost
Hunted by the beast
And that's just in your dreams
The nightmares start
With the alarm clock
Dragging you out
Of a peaceful state
To live death
To breathe hate
Time drags your ambition
Through the mud
It spits you back out
Into an unforgiving world

206 Nothing Is Sacred

Turn the other cheek
But both are scarred
Yeah hey mom
Are you proud of me
For being so dark and twisted
No I know I know
You always told me
To write about
Positive uplifting things
Sorry but it's hard to be positive
When every morning
You're up lifting things
Yes I know I know
That didn't work
I just had to say it
I say a lot of the stupid things
I think up these days
I have to
I'm already a dark twisted soul
On the edge of insanity and slipping
Oh look mom
I'm still the same
Lame corny dork
I always was

Robert Ragan 207

Settle Down

Tried my best to settle down
Gave it all I had to ditch trouble
Yeah that's what I did
Now I swear these people
Gonna make me lose it
And have to do another bid
In the meantime
It's the poetry shadow work
Or a humiliation ritual
I'm putting myself through
Typing everything now
I put down the pen
Scared the internet
Will shut down
And lose it all
When everything
Could be safe
In the pages of notebook
The ink on all those lines Sacred
Sorry I'm just giving it to you
Like I'm thinking it
I don't want problems with anyone
Still I believe in the code
Square the fuck up
Man to man
Everyone around stay out of it
Let em Square the fuck up
Hand to hand
Even though I believe in the code
Don't think for a second
That I won't break it
Catch em sleeping

208 Nothing Is Sacred

Poke em with the baseball bat
Until they wake up
Imagine waking up
And seeing someone ready to
Break your bones and
Make you bleed
Hell they just
Might kill you
I know it's not fair
But life isn't fair either
I respect the code
But at the same time
Fuck the code
Thief over everything else
And you know how
We are with honor
If you love me and
You're good to me
There's nothing
I wouldn't do for you
If you hate me and
You fuck with me
I want to be the one
Who brings all the fear to your life
Sorry my mind is all over the place
I'm just giving it to you
Like the thoughts
Come to me
If you read this thank you
And please pray for me
Wish me luck
Or something motherfucker
I tried my best to settle down

Robert Ragan 209

To stay the fuck out of trouble
Yeah I made that change
I did that
Now I swear these idiots are
Gonna make me lose it
Get locked up again
Because I did something
Fucking stupid

Sometimes It Be Like That

Crack is wack
Actually I'm more
Of a meth guy
Ain't brushed my teeth
In six weeks
Sorry for the breath guy
But thanks for buying
My couch for the fifth time

Karma Is A Motherfucker

Should have smoked
That blunt at my buddies house
Instead we decided to blaze
On the way back home
Sure enough
A car sped up behind us
Bright lights blinding me
When the blue lights came on
My heart literally skipped a beat
Shit I was hoping
To get out of there
With a little
Possession of Marijuana charge
But as soon as they ran my name
I knew they would
Bring the dogs out
In the trunk
Underneath the spare tire
My fate was sealed
My friend with me
I knew he would never squeal
Didn't matter I was going
To take the blame for everything
Later on I was
Sitting inside the cell
With my face buried
In my hands feeling defeated
Thinking I might as well
Make myself comfortable
I knew I would
Be there for awhile
Was already having problems

212 Nothing Is Sacred

With my ol lady
Now she could do
Whatever the Hell
She wanted to
Have motherfuckers I hate
Hanging out all night
Just tell em
The light bill
Plus the water bill
Are both due soon
Oh and I forgot about the WiFi
Sorry bitch let
Everything get cut off
She moved in
With one of them
I still had a good bit
Of time left to do
It hurt finding that
I had nowhere to go
When they finally let me out
Meanwhile not a soul sent
Commissary money
A picky eater
But I had to learn
To force down the slop
When I got out this time
Would I go back to living
The same life or would I stop
These are the questions
I asked myself every day
Only I couldn't answer them
Until I got a breath of fresh free air
Betrayed by everyone

Robert Ragan 213

Crowned a loner
The jail was overcrowded
But in my mind
It was only me in there
Facing all the consequences
Of my actions
If I hadn't lit up that blunt
Oh fuck that
Crooked ass cops
Were going to search my car
No matter what
I mean come on its me
King pusher on the back lot
My name came up
When they ran my tags
Bet the bitches said Jackpot!!!
Let's tear this fucking car apart
Might find some dope or a gun in there
Yeah they got me with the dope
A few fiends were broken hearted
At least they didn't get me
With the pistol
Little tape on the handle revolver
Was back at my place
Word is one of those guys
Hanging out getting high
And fucking my ol lady
Took the gun
Eventually got caught with it
And went to jail
Had him all jammed up
With the serial numbers filed off
I laughed when I heard about it
Thinking karma is a motherfucker

214 Nothing Is Sacred

It definitely is
Every time it comes
To pay me back

That Fucking Loser In Your Inbox

Baby say she want a man
But threatens anyone
Who pops up in her inbox
I don't know where
The fuck you live at
I don't have your number
So how am I supposed
To shoot my shot
Pretty face
Nice body
Damn you're hot
For you me taking the photo
Might not work
Might fuck around and hire a photographer
To take this dick pic
Side note: Any professional female photographers out there
hit me up.
Just kidding I only
Send pics like that
If they're requested
And yes you guessed it
I hardly ever
Send pics like that
Shit I'm a real man
I treat women with respect
So I don't know why
These bitches
Won't have anything
To do with me
The last woman desperate enough
To come out and meet me was like
I thought you said
216 Nothing Is Sacred

You were a real man
But you live in a nasty trash can
You don't have a driver's license
Or a car
What kind of real man are you
She said all that before peeling off
I'm standing there trying
To hit her up on Messenger
And the bitch blocked me
In the middle of driving
She missed out
But if I could
Get your permission
To slide up in your inbox
You could have
Something special with me
All jokes aside
I'm ugly as Hell
Stupid as fuck
I don't have a
Driver's license or a car
And I do live in a trash can
On the bright side I do try
To buy people's love
Had a couple of
Long distance relationships
With women I met on FB
One I sent a necklace ring and bracelet
The other i sent over 400 dollars in cash
Looks like all you gold digging
Harnett County bitches
Really did miss out on me after all
The cash plus all that jewelry

Robert Ragan 217

Just think about all the
Meth and Percoset it would have bought
Sorry baby I'm just rambling
I know you ain't like that
I can tell by the way
You carry yourself on social media
That you can't be one
Of those greedy drug addict ho's
I know you do like
To smoke loud weed though
Trust me baby I've got you
Know where to get some fire
Anyway I'm gonna go now
I hope you're not mad at me
For deciding to go ahead
And send this message
Wait oh shit she just seen it
Damn I hope she's cool
And doesn't block me
Fuck damn
I knew it
She blocked me
Could have got my whole paycheck
Every week
She's got her own money
She never needed anything
From a loser like me anyway
Shit gonna go slit both of my wrists
I'm out

218 Nothing Is Sacred

No Lies About Hope

Another sleepless night
When I talk about it
I can see your wheels turning
Like didn't this dude
Just admit publicly
That he's battling
Meth addiction
Now he's on here
Talking about sleepless nights
Well first of all
I've been clean
For almost a month
Plus tell me this
Was I doing ice in elementary school
When I lay in bed wide awake as a kid
All night worrying about
Not passing
No I wasn't on meth then
Believe it or not
Sometimes I don't sleep for days
High off nothing but loud weed
Mixed with a lot of anxiety and depression
Most of the time
I don't sleep
For being up all night
Worried about how
I'm gonna fuck up
At work the next day
Or maybe it's some irrational fear
Turned mind bending obsession
Like how I'm nothing but a fake

Robert Ragan 219

All that tough talk
And scared to see
A little blood
All that tough talk
And scared to death
I'm gonna have to fight
Sounds like someone
Needs to stop it with
All that tough talk
Always suicidal
Then mortality
Calls my bluff
So soft
I started thinking
Maybe I'll write romance
Make it passionate
Yeah right I'm especially scared
Of commitment and relationships
Maybe I should just write
About nothing but
The everyday fear
I have of simply existing
 Maybe I shouldn't write anything
At least spare myself
That inevitable shame

220 Nothing Is Sacred

Feed My Addiction

I had to hide
Who I really am
With you
Late at night
Come home
Out of breath
You swore
I was out cheating
But I really got
Chased through the woods
After I got caught
Trying to climb
Through someone's window
My clothes ripped
After getting tangled
In briars
At one point I thought
This guy was going
To catch me
I had to kick it
In another gear
And run faster
He finally gave up
So really I
Outran the bastard
But I couldn't share
That part of my life with you
How else do you think
I always had a bag
Of loud weed

Robert Ragan 221

Damn sure won't from working
With my record I couldn't
Get a job anywhere at the time
So to feed my addiction
I had to go out at
All Times Of The Night
Doing a lot of things
I wasn't proud of
Still I laughed and
Bragged about it all
Smoking with my thieving buddies
So I must have not
Been too ashamed of it
With you I had to talk about
Filling out job applications
Our plans for the future
And all that shit
Swear to God
I could have
Come home
Filled with
Bullet wounds
And somehow you would
Connect it to me
Cheating on you
You're fucking with
Some bitch married
Or in a relationship
And her man caught ya'll
Then he shot your sorry ass
Hearing all that bullshit
I'm like fuck all those plans
Bitch I don't want a future with you

222 Nothing Is Sacred

And listen to your paranoid schizophrenic
Shit about me cheating on you
All the time...fuck that
By the way I really did cheat on you
All your investigating
Didn't amount to shit
So it was all a breeze
Talking to you
While laying in her bed
I cheated on you with ease
I definitely couldn't
Share that part
Of my life with you now
Could I
That's why I'm glad
It all didn't work out
I'm glad you got to see
Who I really am
I knew you wouldn't
Like that side of me
Why do you think
I hid it from you
For so long

Joy To The World

With the broken heart
Criminal activity
And mental illness
I don't think about her
As much as I used to
But tonight I wish
I could bring Joy
Back to the world
You made me
The monster I am
Out of nothing but
Depression
Love
And good intentions
The same woman
Who let me watch
A Nightmare On Elm Street
At such a young age
Also made me suffer
Through hours and hours
Of Dirty Dancing
Until I grew
To love it myself
I remember her
Sitting there for hours
Writing poetry in a notebook
A few times
She told me
She was trying
To write a short story
Nothing ever came
From any of it

224 Nothing Is Sacred

The last thing
I remember her writing
Were words on the wall
In her own blood
On my eighteenth birthday.....
My father worked hard
To the bone
I took after him
Just a little bit
But I mainly
Get it all
From my mama
The obsessions
The depression
I have to remind myself
That it's mostly her blood
Running through my veins
The only difference in us
Is that I chased my dreams
And didn't give up
Maybe I'm stupid
For chasing the impossible
Trust me
Ever since you've been gone
I chase it more ways than one
Hope you hear my thoughts
Going down on this page
Just wanted you to know
How you passed on
The love of writing
Now I have
A ton of poetry
To show for all

Robert Ragan 225

The hours I've sat
In front of a notebook
Short stories I've completed
Even novel first drafts
To show how
I took my art more seriously
Than my responsibilities
I have to think
Where would I be
If you had done that to me
Through it all you made me
The monster that I am
Out of nothing but
Depression
Love
And good intentions
On the brightside
You gave me
The passion for words
That makes me
Want to go on
With life
When everything else
Seems hopeless
My whole writing style
The dark
The insanity
I owe it all to you
Mixed with a lot
Of the neighborhood troublemakers
That you said would cause me
To end up in trouble too
You should have known
I'd never amount to much

226 Nothing Is Sacred

After all the times
You had to beg my father
To bail me out of jail
You loved me
And did the best you could
Despite the madness
Because of you
I'll never forget
"If This Is It"
By Huey Lewis & The News
Along with a million other songs
I can't help but remember
I don't think about you
As much as I used to
But tonight
I'd give anything
For the chance
To bring Joy
Back to the world

The Face Of Irresponsibility

Living with my parents
In my thirties
I'd tell em I'm sick
Not going to work today
Mama would buy it
Daddy said
You're still gonna be sick
If you stay here all day
Might as well
Take your ass to work
And get paid for being sick
When I was unemployed
He was the same man
Who'd ask my friends
You know why
Robert won't go out and
Look for a job
They'd ask why
Wait for it
Then laugh like Hell
When my old man said
He's scared he might find one
Oh can't forget this one
When the Lord said Brain
Robert thought he said Rain
And ran under a shelter
Even he would admit
That I hustle and
Bust my ass when I work
He'd say the problem
Is getting him
To get up and go

228 Nothing Is Sacred

Easy for him to say
He was naturally talented
At working on things
He was confident
Me I'm scared to death
Of not performing well
Need constant reassurance
Always asking
Am I doing this right
My father found out
How I always ask that question
He told his friend
Who got me this particular job
Yeah I've noticed he does that
Turning to me he asked
Son when you're with a woman and
You're fucking her
Do you stop and ask her
Am I doing this right
His friend
My boss
Got a big laugh
Out of that
I told myself
I'll fuck his whole job up
Before I ever ask another question
That job wasn't for me anyway
But the next one i got
I told myself
I'm gonna be there every day
Finally force my sperm donor
To eat his words
This would be a win win situation

Robert Ragan 229

I'd get every dollar possible and
Prove him and everyone else
Wrong in the process
It was tough
Some weeks I wasn't there everyday
But I was for the most part
Still I could live another lifetime
And not be half the man
My father was
Never seen him go without a car
He always had to have one
Would drive that bitch to work
Six or seven days a week sometimes
A workaholic
But he still got out and lived life
Had a motorcycle
A couple of fast cars
But what he loved the most
Was going out riding horses
Only time I ever
Seen the man without a job
Was after he nearly
Got his foot ripped off
While riding a horse
He hated sitting at home
Doing nothing but eating
And watching television all day
Behind on the bills
His number one priority
Was getting back to his job
Against my mother's wishes
He went right back
To riding horses
Thinking back now

230 Nothing Is Sacred

I admire that so much
Wish I had half that fire
Gotta a little flame in my heart
But it never burns
The way his did
Despite being responsible and
Actually getting out living life
He definitely had shortcomings as well
For instance he ended up
Quitting school at an early age
To go out and work
In hot tobacco fields
So he grew up
Barely knowing how to read
After all the times
He made me the punchline
You know one day me
The wannabe writer
Had to crack on him
About not knowing how to read
He said maybe I can't read or write
But I get out here and make a living
How much money are you making
Reading and writing in all those notebooks
Maybe he couldn't read or write
But he could roast the Hell out of me
And talk more knowledge
Than I ever begin to in all my notebooks
He told me stories
About those hot tobacco fields
How the boss left
A bunch of teenage boys in charge
My daddy said

If he got tired and got behind
They would go in the woods
And pick switches to beat him with
He was scared to say anything
But of course my grandmother
Eventually noticed
The marks all over his back
She went to the farmer and told him
What those boys were doing
And they never did it again
My father told me
When he got older
He always thought about
Going out and finding these guys
And beating the fuck
Out of every one of em
One at a time one on one
Then he said
What happened happened
No use in trying to get revenge
He said, besides they taught me
Not to get behind
You think I'm good
At working on everything
But I worry about messing up too.
He said I just face it
And do the best I can everyday
Hell he was never the type
To do any kind of drugs
But I can remember my old man
Going out getting drunk
Coming home with his eyebrow
Busted wide open bleeding
Telling me

232 Nothing Is Sacred

He got in a fight at the bar
I know my father even had
Wild nights with other women
While my mother was locked up
In a mental institution
No saint she sin first
Behind those walls of insanity
Oh my God
I feel like REM
Oh no I've said too much
But I've definitely said enough
Anyway I could go on and on
About my Dad
He was also very talented
At shooting pool
So much that he gambled
On the table
Both won and lost
That was the only thing
He was ever able to teach me
Got pretty good at the game
But never good enough to beat him
Wish I was half the man he was

Robert Ragan 233

Free Gavin

If anyone had the right
To never speak to me again
It would be my son
He wasn't in another state
So what was my excuse
For not being in his life
I had no excuse
Just the dark truth
How many nights
Did I pass up my time with them
Leaving them with my parents
As I went out...
Got fucked up and chased women
Through it all I'd say
He has the right
To hate me more
But he doesn't
He understands
He doesn't judge
He forgives
And even though
I was never there for him
He still loves me
He still wants me
To be a part of his life
It's all up to me
Will I continue
To choose this nonsense
Or finally get my shit right
Don't I owe it to him..
Damn right I owe it to him
When those doors open

234 Nothing Is Sacred

That's when it has to start
I've got to do something
Baby steps from the father
I never had all the answers

Grand Baby

So pathetic
Soon I will
Try to write
A parody of me
To All The Girls
I Mistakenly Thought
I Loved Before
Until then
I'm trying to solve
The mystery
Of why
My own daughter
Has refused to
Speak to me
For over a year
Last time we talked
We laughed and
Got along great
Then suddenly nothing
I message her mother
Who says
She wouldn't speak to me
If she didn't absolutely have to
Lately I've started thinking
Her mother is
Probably helping her
Cover up something
But what could it be
Then it hit me
OH Hell No
So I send her mother a message
Out of the blue I might add saying
236 Nothing Is Sacred

I know you're covering up
For Miranda's pregnancy
I don't know why ya'll trying
To keep my Grand Baby from me
Luckily she got the joke
And said she got a great laugh
Me at this point
I'm just trying
To joke about it
Just to deal with it
Not like I'm
Father of the year or anything
Not when I have
A son closer to me
Who I also never see
Anyway just to follow up
On my joke
Yesterday I talked to
Her mother again
And I messaged saying
I don't know when
Ya'll gonna come clean
And tell me about
My Grand Baby
Probably be in college
Before I find out about it

I Wouldn't Forgive Me Either

Know time has passed
Every second you were
In the back of my mind
Like I'm not doing
What I'm supposed
To be doing in life
I'm not a man
A man takes care
Of his responsibilities
Most times
Putting himself last
I guess I'm just immature and selfish
It's not like I'm out here
Living my best life
If I was I'd make sure
You were living yours too
Honestly this is the worst life
I wouldn't ever want this for you
Even the best for you
Isn't good enough
I wish I could steal the sky
And give you a piece of Heaven
Really I just wish
I could give you
Whatever it is
You want in life
For all the times
I wasn't in your life

238 Nothing Is Sacred

Your Mind Games

I've been doing good
In moving on
Changing my thought process
In order to avoid your memory
But like I said before
I like playing Block Unblock too
Only this time I'm able to get the news
Without unblocking you
Got a couple of screenshots
Saw you posted about...
Red flags
Chicken nuggets and
Pizza rolls
Immediately I was overcome with joy
Like she's still thinking about me
She really misses me
Was so close to unblocking you
Then sending a message saying
Your prince is still here Beautiful
For once I was glad to have OCD
Being it's relationship subtype
Forced me to slow down this happiness
To obsess over it and pick it all apart
As soon as I started within a few seconds
I told myself somehow it had to be a trap
I'm nothing but an ugly peasant
So obviously you had to be
Talking about a new prince
Wrapped in red flags
Who could also appreciate your love for
Pizza rolls and chicken nuggets

Robert Ragan 239

Basically Immature foods
That grown adults don't eat on a regular basis
Yeah that had to be it...
Then again how lame would that be
To joke about two relationships in a row
Plus you hardly ever post anything public
So it made more sense
That you thought I'd be stalking and
See these posts
You just knew I'd see them
Reach out and prove
That I still care
So you could block me again
Well not this time and never again
And yes it was Immature and undermining
Of me to have someone spy on your posts
We are both far too old
To play all these childish games
The thing is I'm playing them
Because I still care about you
You're playing them
Because you want to hurt me
Because you don't want lose
So of course you still think about me
But you don't miss me at all
If you did you have my number
And you would call
Anyway nice try
But I win
Because I choose
To keep you blocked
And play from the outside
Looking in

240 Nothing Is Sacred

Truth Be Told

Life of crime no
My life is a crime
Seen better people go
While I continue to waste air
I turn back to all this
Trying to avoid real life
But while I'm talking about my father
Let me tell you about the father
 I am
Never really there
For either one of my kids
They've both had to face
Terrible things
Neither one of them
Should have ever been exposed to
I could have been there
If I was a real fucking man
And handled my business
Like I'm supposed to
Hell I can barely take care of myself
My daughter decided
She doesn't ever want
To talk to me again
And my son has the right
To do the same
Can't stand letting
Down blood
I gave my last name
Like I said I'll never be
Half the man
My father was

Truth be told
I was a terrible son
Not to mention
I'm even worse
As a father

Say Never Again

Begged them to stay
Only to watch lovers
Walk out the door
Every time I say never again
Believe it when someone tells you
Never say never
Soon some other doll
Will enter the picture
I'll take her words to heart
She too will leave me devastated
How much could it possibly hurt
After I've sat watching
As cell doors slammed shut
How much of me can it take
After seeing my father
On his deathbed
After never getting to see
My mother on hers
They can break my heart
But it's broken much worse
By my dreams dying
When the words weren't good enough
Yeah they can break my heart
But only the part of it that loves
The part that somehow gives me
The strength to go on
Is still beating in my chest
Never say Never no...
Say Never Again

Witness Love Contradict Itself

A.M hours breed crime
Swallow dreams whole
Whose soul is it anyway
I belonged to you
When the power
Got turned off
And you went back
To your mother's
I belonged to you
Even though I made
Our place a flop trailer
I was always yours at heart
Such a broad
Only you knew nothing
About daylight
Hidden away in your tomb
Until the sun goes down
Acting as if I should
Drop to my knees
And praise the Lord
That you finally
Decided to wake up
Ain't you about an entitled fucking brat
Titty and pacifier toddler
Go back to fucking bed
If you think I should be
Grateful that you're awake
 Oh what happened to your cigarettes
you smoked em all
So now you want
To smoke the rest of mine too
Hell no I'm not getting up

244 Nothing Is Sacred

Go get your own Mountain Dew
I didn't see you get up
To make breakfast
Pack a lunch or anything
Before I left for work
So why should I do anything for you
At this point
You're more of a roommate
Than a lover
And you ain't paid
The first goddamn bill
So technically
I have the right
To kick you
The fuck out
You don't like my
Trashy flop trailer anyway
So what if you
Fall through the floor
It's a roof over your head right
No you're not going
To drop dead from a spider bite
Oh and don't say a word
About me harboring fugitives
At my place
You let your father stay
After he escaped
From the mental institution
So fuck you
Can't carry or pull your weight
Sad for a skin and bones princess
One step away from the dead
Really you make me sick

Robert Ragan 245

Especially after I devoted
My entire life
To being with you
Even more when I
Literally belonged to you
During those A.M hours
With your fangs
Sunk deep into my dreams
My soul was always yours
Go running back
To your mom's now
Tell her we had a huge fight
Tell her how much you hate me
And how you're never
Getting back with me again
Lies watch their backs
Coming from the
Mouths of unstable hosts
They hope you all forget
Knowing none of you
Are truly capable of forgiveness
Now that smoke fills the room
I am nothing
I belong to no one
When it all clears
You won't get me back
Not with you
Not for hurting me
I'll be the darkest chapter
The one unresolved
The one that keeps you awake
At night

246 Nothing Is Sacred

All Went Wrong

I've been the fake
Stabbed friends
In the back
Hating it
The whole time
Thinking I'm gonna
Come back and make it right
I've also stood up for them
Had their backs
With no blade in my pocket
Kept secrets that I knew
Would divide our whole group
Had a friend facing three strikes
So I told him
Give me the bag
When we got pulled over
But they don't remember
Any of sacrifices that I made
They just remember that
I was ruthless on my mission
No one was safe
Breaking into my parents place
Stealing my mom's pills
Now I'm preaching
Joy To The World
What a fake
I was a terrible son
Even worse as a father
The whole time
I fucking hate this
Thinking I'm gonna come back

Robert Ragan 247

And make it right
It all went wrong so easily

248 Nothing Is Sacred

With Words

Think you can
Tear me down
With words
Not when I've had friends
To tell me
To get lost
Not when I've had a woman I love
Tell me it's over and
To pack my stuff and
Get the fuck out of her house
Think I give a fuck
What you pussies
Have to say about me
How's it feel
All of you
Only cool in
Your own circle
Everyone outside of it
We all see you're all
A bunch of hypocrites
Like everyone on their side
Can make offensive statements
And it's all good no problem
Then let someone outside the circle
Say the exact same thing
And these motherfuckers
Get their panties twisted
And go into an uproar
The real ones just laugh
And the sheep follow these bitches
So think you can tear me down with words

Robert Ragan 249

Think I give a fuck what you pussies
Have to say about me
I've heard my daughter
Say she hated me
Heard my father say
He never wanted
A writer for a son
They meant for it to at the time
And man that shit really hurt me
So think you can
Tear me down with words
Man I don't think you can
Maybe if I respected you
But believe me I don't
I think you're the lowest
Of the fucking low
All your little friends
They're all sinking with you
I hope you all know
Now don't let me
Hear a peep
Out of you about this
If so it means
I've torn you down
With words
It means you care
What I have to say about you

250 Nothing Is Sacred

Other Way Around

Cut your hands
On the sharpest star
Red raindrops
As you bled
From the sky
I remember the day
You flew away
How we both said goodbye
You were sick
Of being on the run
Your legs were tired
You were out of breath
Mentally you just had
No motivation left
But then a surge of energy
Gave you wings
Now you party with the sun
The Holy Ghost and The Father
Baby the shit
You write me
From jail
Is outrageous
Yes I'll send you
Money for Ramen
And another notebook
You just keep
Filling up those pages
Yes I talked to your lawyer
He said it's not looking good
But don't give up hope
Baby you'll be alright

Robert Ragan 251

If any of those jailbird bitches
Try to fuck with you
I'll send enough Commissary money
For you to put a price
On their pretty little heads
Take care and you'll never know
How much this means to me
That's what I wrote her
Really what she did
Does mean a lot to me
It's means she's
Locked up and I'm not
It means I'm the one
Out fucking around
With other women
Then lying to her about it
Instead of the other way around
And that's how it should be

252 Nothing Is Sacred

Mirror Glass Hour

Wow who would have ever thought
Me giving parenting tips
This is for the parents
Who ask their kids
To piss for em
Wow you're setting a
Fine example
While I'm at it though
Don't expect me
To diss you and
Say something negative
About your children
As a matter of fact
I think you should grow up
Act like an adult and
Give them time to be children
You already had your childhood
Don't let your kids
Grow up before you do
Another thing I'm not talking about
Killing your children for God's sake
But don't let me
Catch em outside unattended
Gonna fuck around and
Spin the block and
Leave everything you have
Filled with bullet holes
Everything you love too
See what the fuck I mean
You sound fucking pathetic
Saying those type of things

Robert Ragan 253

If it was me
I'm shooting your kids lights out
On the basketball goal out front
make em
Feel bad when they can't stop
The fade away
Just to mess with em
Been a terrible dad
For over 20 years now
Sadly I'm not in contention
To win Father Of The Year
This year either
What am I talking about
I'll never win it
More for lack of money
Never lack of heart
Anyway at least I know
That you'll never
Win it either
Night before your drug test
Handing you're kid a cup
You could have given them so much more
But you were more concerned
With getting fucked up
Giving your dopedealers all your extra money
Bet their kids had the latest
In back to school fashion
Bet their kids had a great Christmas

254 Nothing Is Sacred

Satanic Panic In A Small Town

Last published in chalk
It was midnight
In the cul-de-sac
Above the influence
Of something toxic
My system was shocked
On the asphalt
I wrote
It's all the asses fault
Along with other things
That made no sense at all
I write like this and call it cryptic
The next morning
The whole neighborhood watch program
Was on the scene
They called the cops
Who said it was just
An immature teenager
Scribbling nonsense
Hey that hurt
But at least I
Had em way off track
Can you believe
The people in the community
All said it was the work of a Satanist
A Satanist...man I didn't say shit
About the fucking devil
Just goes to show
How anything they don't
Understand is evil
I couldn't go back to

Robert Ragan 255

That particular housing development
But I had something else for em
Two weeks later right down the road
In front of the old Parker farm
I got busy with the chalk
In the driveway leading up to their shop
I wrote in huge letters
This isn't over
Until we have the head of every goat
After that we will sacrifice
All of your children
Our dark master
Wants fresh blood
It was funny as Hell at first
Causing Satanic panic
In this small town
But then my scrupulosity
started acting up
It was God's way of telling me
You're gonna burn
In the hottest pits of Hell
For using the devil
To play a joke
On these hardworking believers
Every time I thought about it
I either got a headache
Or had really bad chest pains
I had to make it right
Tell em all it was
An immature grown man
Scribbling nonsense
And that the Lord punished me
For doing such a childish thing
But where would I leave this message

256 Nothing Is Sacred

After the last writing
The cops took it seriously
Out all night patrolling
What I really need to do
Is stay the fuck
Off all the dope
If I hadn't been
Fucked up out of my mind
I would have never done
Such a silly stupid thing
Years have went by
I never did chalk
Out the words to make it right
Things settled down
But a lot of the older town folks
Still believe there's
Evil Satanist amongst us
Stalking the community
Damn I'm so
Ashamed of myself
What a fucking dweeb
A loser with no hope indeed
What's worse is
I told you about this on a
 Sunday morning.

Robert Ragan 257

Best Believe

Oblivious
That's how you
Made me look
Going places
Seeing people
But they'd all seen you
With someone else
I didn't know at first
But you can best believe
I always expected the worst
It's what I got
It's all I got
From you
But you can best believe
Two could play that game
I played it well
Didn't want to exploit
Anyone's weakness
But I had to get with
Your best friend
You were away
On getting your grooves
I was sleeping with her
And she told me
All the moves
You were making
Whose oblivious now
Obviously not me
Plus I'll never forget your tears
When you finally found out
Was it so shocking
To learn

258 Nothing Is Sacred

You got beat
At your own game
You can best believe
You couldn't believe it
And you can best believe
I fucking loved it

Bow To No One

Wear the thorns
Sacred one
Come apart
You're dying
To see
The other world
Don't you remember
I can take you there
Take you back there
Lipstick on glass
Viles filled
To the brim
With delight
Oh you don't
Remember that night
I can take you there
Take you back there
Just come apart with me
Fall to pieces
All I ever wanted
Was to put
You back together
Make a brand new you
A you that would
Love me and only me
A you that I would
Love unconditionally
It's sad
But we can
Never get it back
We can never get it back
But you can best believe

260 Nothing Is Sacred

I fought for it
I bled for it
Cried for it
Begged for it
But we just couldn't
Get it back
It couldn't work
I'm still coming apart
I'm still falling to pieces
No new me
Just the same old me
That loves you and only you
The same ol me
That you could never
Love unconditionally
But it's alright
It's all okay
I understand and
Still want you to shine
It's possible
If you put
Your mind to it
You can escape those chains
I want to bring you back
I hate where you are now
I can take you somewhere better
Take you back with me

The Official Sacred Name

Our thoughts
On the same page
The ink would bleed insane
Imagine us
Kicking it
Philosophers and
Great artist
Spoken of
As we're smoking up
It would be
Fucking outrageous
Us together on
The same canvas
Picking all our colors carefully
Someday I want to bring you back
I'll buy us a cheap motel room
And we can get wild
Paint and write all night
Write and paint all night
It would be so awesome
Who else but us
Loves art to the death
Many do
But not quite like us
I want to bring that you
Back someday
Gonna break my heart
If I never get to
Always remember
Your name
Was the first one
I ever held Sacred

262 Nothing Is Sacred

I'm going to bring
You back someday
Yes you will make it

Robert Ragan 263

Save You Somehow

One more time
For the shadows
I hate how they
Make a mess of you
Made you come apart
They try to take all of you
But I'm going to take
The rest of you
And love you
With all my heart
First I'm going
To bring you back
Take you back with me
To a place
Where we'll learn
To play mind games
With the shadows
I'll be in your nightmares
Both of us frozen stiff
Unable to move
But you'll know
I'm with you
I'm with you right now
But you don't know it
I'm with you
But I still have to bring you back
When I met you
It was pixie cut
With a bandana
I'll never forget
The way your eyes glowed
When you were fascinated

264 Nothing Is Sacred

By something
No I'll be in your nightmares
But I will break free
I have to save you
In order to save me
As far as reality
I've got to bring you
Back someday
It will destroy me
If I never get to
For your name
Is always Sacred
Gonna bring you back
And yes you will make it
We'll finally make it

About The Author

Robert Ragan, crime writer and poet, is currently working on his fourth short story collection *All Times of the Night*. You can find his work at cool places like *Switchblade Magazine*, *Close to the Bone*, *Bristol Noir*, *Synchronized Chaos* and *Punk Noir Magazine*.

The
Independent
Fiction
Alliance

**A Coalition of
Writers and Publishers
Committed
to the
Freedom
of
Speech**

www.independentfictionalliance.com

www.ingramcontent.com/pod-product-compliance
Lightning Source LLC
LaVergne TN
LVHW041315080426
835513LV00008B/461